VEGANS GO
NUTS

CELEBRATE PROTEIN-PACKED NUTS AND SEEDS WITH MORE THAN 100 DELICIOUS PLANT-BASED RECIPES

CELINE STEEN & JONI MARIE NEWMAN

FAIR WINDS

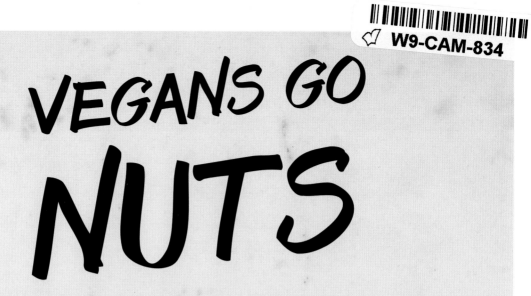

Quarto is the authority on a wide range of topics.

Quarto educates, entertains and enriches the lives of our readers—enthusiasts and lovers of hands-on living.

www.QuartoKnows.com

First published in the United States of America in 2016 by
Fair Winds Press, an imprint of
Quarto Publishing Group USA Inc.
100 Cummings Center
Suite 406-L
Beverly, Massachusetts 01915-6101
Telephone: (978) 282-9590
Fax: (978) 283-2742
QuartoKnows.com
Visit our blogs at QuartoKnows.com

20 19 18 17 16   1 2 3 4 5

ISBN: 978-1-59233-725-5

Digital edition published in 2016
eISBN: 978-1-63159-170-9

Library of Congress Cataloging-in-Publication Data available

Book and Cover Design: Megan Jones Design
Cover Image: Celine Steen
Page Layout: Megan Jones Design
Photography: Celine Steen (www.celinesteen.com)

Printed and bound in China

The information in this book is for educational purposes only. It is not intended to replace the advice of a physician or medical practitioner. Please see your health care provider before beginning any new health program.

In loving memory of
Betsy Gammons.

CONTENTS

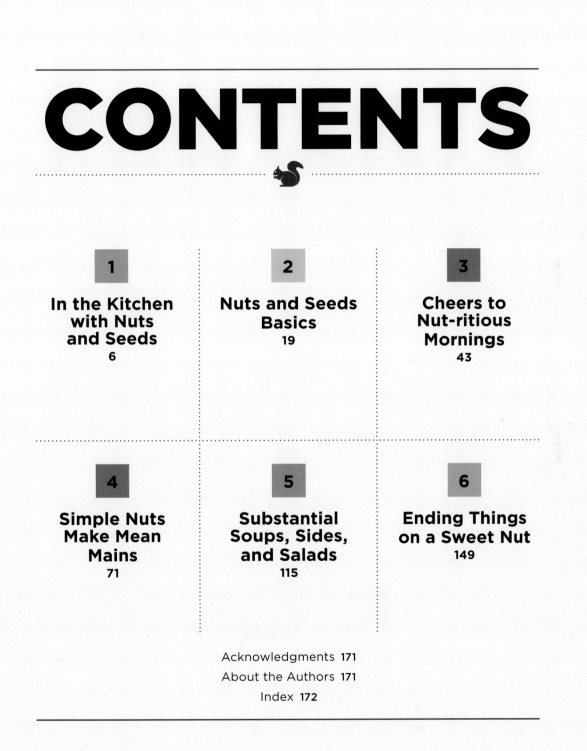

IN THE KITCHEN WITH NUTS AND SEEDS

Nuts and seeds are some of the world's most perfect foods! These little nutrition-packed nuggets of energy are as important a source of food for people around the world today as they have been for centuries.

Thanks to the prevalence of plant-based diets and a growing focus on health, nuts are more popular than ever. They are rich in protein, vitamins, minerals, and essential unsaturated and monounsaturated fats. Seeds are no slouches either, with a high protein content, B vitamins, minerals, essential unsaturated and monounsaturated fats, and dietary fibers.

Two long-term Harvard studies followed 120,000 participants over thirty years. What did they find? "We found that people who ate nuts every day lived longer, healthier lives than people who didn't eat nuts," said study coauthor Dr. Frank Hu, professor of nutrition and epidemiology at the Harvard School of Public Health.

Many people think nuts are fattening due to their high fat and calorie content. The Harvard studies also found that those who ate nuts daily were *less* likely to gain weight because nuts are high in protein and fiber, leaving you feeling full and satisfied.

Needless to say, we're not speaking of nuts from a can, roasted in oil, and loaded with salt, high-fructose corn syrup, and hard-to-pronounce (or digest!) ingredients. Nuts and seeds are most beneficial when enjoyed in their raw or dry-roasted, unsalted form. Aside from that, it doesn't even matter which type of nut you grab—they're all healthy!

Nuts are extremely versatile and can be turned into flours (also known as *meals*), milks, and butters. They can also be combined with other ingredients to make cheeses, sauces, spreads, and more. Can any other food pull that off? We think not. Before we get to the recipes, let's dive in to all that nuts can do and explore how to best prepare them!

THE NUT AND SEED GLOSSARY

What's the difference between a nut and a seed anyway? Technically, true nuts are fruits, but it gets a little tricky. All true nuts are also seeds, but not all seeds are nuts. And not all seeds come from fruits; some come from vegetables and others from flowers. Let us explain.

Botanically speaking, a true nut is a hard-shelled pod that contains both the *fruit and seed* of the plant. In this case, the fruit does not open to release the seed. Examples of true nuts include chestnuts, hazelnuts, and acorns.

A seed, on the other hand, is simply the embryonic plant surrounded by a food source and encased in a shell. Some seeds, such as sunflower seeds and pumpkin seeds, need the shell removed from the seed before eating. Others, such as poppy or sesame, do not require shell removal prior to consumption.

To add to the confusion, there is also a type of fruit known as a stone fruit or *drupe*. Drupes are composed of a fleshy exterior surrounding a shell that, in turn, contains a seed. Some common drupes are peaches, plums, olives, and cherries. Deep inside these fruits are seeds that we refer to as the pit. While we often throw away the pits, other drupes, such as walnuts, almonds, and pecans, are more valued for their tasty seeds than the fruit that surrounds it. They're therefore mistakenly referred to as nuts, when really they are seeds.

You need fat as part of your diet, and eating nuts helps ensure that your fat intake comes from healthy unsaturated fat rather than the harmful saturated fats found in meats, dairy, and other animal products.

To avoid all of this confusion, the term *culinary nuts* refers to all nuts and seeds that are used for cooking or eating. For further clarification, we added the type (nut, seed, or drupe) next to the description of each in the list that follows.

As a general rule, culinary nuts are great sources of protein, fiber, vitamin E, B-complex vitamins, heart-healthy fats, and essential minerals such as copper and manganese. You need fat as part of your diet, and eating nuts helps ensure that your fat intake comes from healthy unsaturated fat rather than the harmful saturated fats found in meats, dairy, and other animal products.

Most nuts and seeds are pretty common and widely available. If your local grocer has a good bulk section, you will be served well. It's also easy to find online resources for quality bulk nuts and seeds. And, while you've most likely heard of and used most of what's on the list to follow, we did include a few exotic varieties and thought we would share a little bit about each type of nut and seed we will be using in the book.

Almonds: drupe. A real favorite among vegans and snackers around the world, almonds provide heart-healthy protein, B vitamins, calcium, potassium, iron, fiber, mono- and polyunsaturated fats. Almonds are used in both sweet and savory dishes from almond milk to almond butter, marzipan, and vegan cheese. You can find them roasted, salted, smoked, sliced, slivered, blanched, pressed into oil, or ground into flour. There's not a whole lot this nut can't do! We use raw, whole almonds the most. We also use blanched slivered or sliced almonds in this book, and smoked almonds are a favorite for snacking. In the United States most almonds are pasteurized to help prevent salmonella contamination. The Food and Drug Administration (FDA) permits companies to label these almonds as raw provided that "their composition does not fundamentally change" when they are pasteurized.

Brazil nuts: seed. Brazil nuts are native to the Amazon in South America where they grow in trees that tower above the rest. Each tree grows about 300 pods, each containing about 25 to 30 kernels, per growing season. Each kernel is encompassed by a hard brown shell that protects the large creamy, white, meaty, nut inside. These nuts are high in monounsaturated fatty acids, and are a great source of selenium, vitamin E, and B-complex vitamins such as thiamine, riboflavin, and niacin. Brazil nut oil is clear yellow in color, and it has a pleasantly sweet smell and taste. It can be used in cooking, and as a carrier oil for massage and aromatherapy. Brazil nuts are fairly common and should be available in most grocery stores.

Cashews: seed. A real superhero in the world of nuts. Creamy, fatty, and neutral in flavor, cashews are a favorite in the vegan kitchen. Cashews are lower in fat than other nuts, and are high in copper, magnesium, and zinc. Because of their soft, almost spongy texture, when soaked or boiled they are perfect for blending into milk, cheese, ice cream, Alfredo-type sauces, and many other foods. It's best to buy them raw and whole, and cheapest to buy them in bulk whenever possible.

Chestnuts: nut. The ugly duckling of the culinary nut world. Although safe to eat when raw, they are quite bitter and astringent. And, unlike other nuts, chestnuts are not high in protein or fat. The majority of the calories in chestnuts come from carbohydrates, and the starchy meat of the roasted nut is similar to that of a baked potato. Chestnuts have value in tradition as they are fondly roasted over open fires during winter holidays. They are also boiled, baked, or fried with sugars, syrups, and other flavors to make sweet pastes and other confections. Chestnuts can be purchased roasted and ready-to-eat in jars or hermetically sealed packs. Fresh chestnuts should be treated more like vegetables and fruits than nuts when it comes to their storage. To keep them fresh for a few weeks, pack them and store them in the refrigerator set with high relative humidity.

> Chia seeds are a great source of omega-3 fatty acids—in fact, chia is one of the richest sources of them in the plant world.

Chia: seed. Available in white or black, chia seeds can absorb up to ten times their weight in liquid. They are a perfect ingredient to add to smoothies, sauces, dips, and spreads as a natural thickener and nutritional booster. Chia seeds are a great sources of omega-3 fatty acids—in fact, chia is one of the richest sources of them in the plant world. Store chia seeds in the refrigerator in an airtight container, such as a mason jar.

Coconuts: fruit. Though coconut is technically a botanical fruit, the United States FDA requires any food containing coconut to be labeled as containing nuts. While we are fans of coconut and we use it as an ingredient, we focus on traditional nuts and seeds in this book. We are not using coconut as the main "nut" in any recipes.

Flaxseeds: seed. Flaxseeds can be eaten whole or ground; however, the shiny shell of these tiny nutritional beasts is not digestible by humans when whole. In order to get the most nutrition out of flax, it's best to consume it ground or milled into flour. Flax is high in omega-3's and lignans, which are fiber-like compounds that have added antioxidant benefits. Flax can be purchased whole or already ground. If purchasing ground, make sure to store it in an airtight container in the refrigerator or freezer. Ground flax has a high oil content. The oil is where all the awesome alpha-Linolenic acid—the primary omega-3 fatty acid in flax—is hiding. The oil can cause flaxseeds to spoil quickly. If buying whole, grind the seeds yourself in a high-powered blender or spice grinder right before using. Add ground flax to baked goods, smoothies, and cookies; stir into oatmeal; or sprinkle over salads. Studies have shown that cooking this seed does little to nothing to change its nutritional profile.

Hazelnuts: nut. Also known as filberts or cobnuts, hazelnuts are sweet and earthy in flavor. They contain more folate than any other nut, and they are high in copper, manganese, and fiber. They are a favorite because they pair so well with chocolate and other confections, and they are often used in baked goods, candies, and as a flavoring in coffee. Hazelnuts are available shelled, unshelled, salted, sweetened, or ground. Try to buy raw nuts without the shell (that shell is a tough one to crack!) instead of processed ones. They should appear bright brownish-yellow in color, uniform in size, and feel heavy in your hand. Hazelnuts in the shell can be stored in cool dry place for years. Store nuts without the shell in an airtight container in the refrigerator or freezer to prevent them from going rancid. Fun fact alert! Ferrero, the company that manufactures Nutella (not vegan) utilizes 25 percent of the world's hazelnuts annually.

> Hemp is considered by many to be the safest, most digestible, balanced, natural, and complete source of protein (10 g in just 3 tablespoons [30 g]!), amino acids, and essential omega-3 fatty acids found anywhere in nature.

Hemp hearts: seed. Hemp hearts are hemp seeds with the shells removed. Some people refer them as shelled hemp seeds and some as hemp hearts. For the purposes of this book, we use the raw hearts without any shells. The flavor is nutty, rich, and adds a buttery note to recipes. Sprinkle them on salads, tacos, or sandwiches. Blend them into smoothies. Stir them into sauces and scrambles. Hemp is considered by many to be the safest, most digestible, balanced, natural, and complete source of protein (10 g in just 3 tablespoons [30 g]!), amino acids, and essential omega-3 fatty acids found anywhere in nature. Hemp seeds are gaining in popularity, and you should be able to find them in most supermarkets and in any health food store.

Macadamia nuts: seed. Macadamia nuts are the fattiest of all culinary nuts. Although they have a higher fat content and lower protein profile, they are also very high in B vitamins, and a great source of calcium, iron, magnesium, manganese, and zinc. Their tough outer shell protects a soft white seed that is buttery in texture, with a slightly sweet taste. Macadamias are rather expensive and, due to their high oil content, can turn rancid quickly. We suggest only buying as many as you need for a recipe, to avoid waste. And be careful if you have companion animals, as macadamias are toxic to pets.

Peanuts: legume. Though it's not technically a nut, we let this flavor-packed bad boy participate in this book. Not only does the world's favorite legume taste fantastic on a sandwich, this little guy is also a nutritional powerhouse! These heart-healthy and antioxidant-rich beans are a great source of biotin, copper, and protein. They are great as a snack, made into peanut butter, blended into sauces, chopped and sprinkled on sundaes, boiled, roasted, fried, or toasted. Peanuts impart a familiar flavor, as well as depth, to just about anything you add them to. We like to buy shelled, unsalted, dry-roasted peanuts for the majority of the recipes in this book. On occasion we buy whole peanuts in the shell for boiling or snacking, and raw Spanish peanuts for when we want complete control over the flavor profile in certain dishes. Peanuts are inexpensive and easy to find at just about any market.

Pecans: drupe. Also not technically a nut, pecans actually are part of the drupe family. Buttery-tasting pecans are most commonly used in dessert-type foods, but they also taste outstanding sprinkled over wintery, rugged salads, or on top of your morning oatmeal and more. On the nutritional front, it's good to know that pecans are loaded with bone-friendly manganese, protein, and unsaturated fats.

Pine nuts: seed. One of the costliest seeds on the market due to the painstaking harvesting process, pine nuts are most commonly used in dry-roasted form in pesto and Mediterranean-style dishes. It's been reported that some people experience what is known as pine mouth, a bitter taste which appears a couple of days after ingestion. It remains relatively unclear what the exact cause for this phenomenon is, although it has been speculated that the source of the pine nuts might be the reason behind it. As far as nutrition goes, pine nuts boast a generous amount of dietary fiber (5 g per cup [135 g]) and protein (18 g per cup [135 g]).

Pistachios: drupe. Used primarily as a snacking nut, pistachios are nutty, yet pleasantly sweet in taste with a fruity aroma. They are a good source of phenolic antioxidants and just a handful of pistachios a day helps you reach your daily recommended levels of minerals, vitamins, and protein. Pistachios make a great snack. They are also regularly used in ice creams and confections, such as halva, baklava, and nougats. Roasted and crushed, they are awesome sprinkled onto salads, sundaes, and yogurts. They can be purchased in their shells or with the shells removed. The flesh should be light green in color and the seed itself should be coated in a thick magenta-colored skin. Most pistachios are now harvested by machine, and it is no longer necessary to dye them, other than to appease those who are used to snacking on the finger-staining treat.

Fun Fact! In years past, it was common to dye pistachios bright red or green to hide the stains on the shells caused by human hands.

Poppy seeds: seed. These tiny seeds are about one-eighth the size of a sesame seed, and they do not need to have their hulls removed to be enjoyed (thank goodness!). They are generally black in color, although white varieties are available in specialty shops. The flavor is nutty and will be intensified if roasted or gently fried to release their aromatic essential oils. With uses across the culinary spectrum, poppy seeds are a popular ingredient in rolls, breads, muffins, cakes, and other baked goods. Sprinkled into salads, puréed into a paste, or blended into milks, poppy seeds are used in cuisines around the world. And yes, ingesting poppy seeds can cause a false positive in tests for opiates— so lay off the muffins and bagels before your next drug test!

Pumpkin seeds (a.k.a. pepitas): seed. Referred to as *pumpkin seeds* when the shells are intact, and *pepitas* when the shells have been removed, we love this seed for its many uses. Pumpkin seeds (as well as the seeds from other squashes, such as butternut) can be seasoned and roasted with the edible shell intact. They are a great source of zinc, which is concentrated in the endosperm coating that is attached to the shell. The oil from pumpkin seeds is valued for its microbial and antifungal properties. Pepitas can be enjoyed as is, sprinkled onto salads or added into soups, and as an ingredient in multi-grain breads and rolls. We like to buy them raw and toast as needed for recipes.

Sesame seeds: seed. Popular as a topping, blended into a paste (tahini), or pressed into oil, sesame seeds are the most popular edible seed in the world. They have a high drought resistance and can be grown in areas where many other crops would fail. With a higher oil content than any other seed, sesame is often grown as an oilseed. The most popular variety is white, which is actually the sesame seed with its hull removed. Many other colors including tan, gold, brown, reddish, gray, and black are also available, and they have subtly different flavor profiles. With a rich, nutty flavor, this seed is popular in cuisines all over the world. Sesame seeds are used in sweet and savory preparations. They can be purchased just about anywhere, and the hulled seeds should be stored in an airtight container in the refrigerator.

Sunflower seeds: seed. Inexpensive and delicious, sunflower seeds can be roasted while still in their shell, making them a messy, yet fun, snack. Once removed from the shell, sunflower kernels have many culinary uses. They are also a very good source of high-quality amino acids, such as tryptophan, which are essential for growth, especially in children. Toasted, roasted, raw, boiled, or fried, add sunflower seeds to fruit and vegetable salads, dressings, casseroles, baked goods, or sprinkle over green salads, rice dishes, and stir-fries. Sunflower seed butter makes an excellent alternative for those with peanut or tree nut allergies.

Walnuts: drupe. Walnuts have a reputation as a symbol of intellectuality due to their uncanny resemblance to the human brain. They are rich in antioxidants, vitamin E, and iron. Just a handful a day will help you reach your daily recommended dosage of many vitamins and minerals, as well as protein. Walnuts are a popular ingredient in cookies, chocolates, and cakes. They are also enjoyed mixed into savory dishes, such as oatmeal, salads, stir-fries, and pasta. Walnut oil has a nutty aroma with excellent astringent properties. It keeps skin moisturized and protected from dryness. The oil is also popular for cooking, and it is used as carrier oil in massage and aromatherapy.

NUT BUTTERS, OILS, POWDERS, MILKS, AND MORE

While we provide basic recipes for making your own nut butters and milks, there are certainly instances when store-bought varieties find their way into our kitchens simply out of convenience. On a recent trip to the local health food store we found almond, sunflower, cashew, hazelnut, and of course, peanut butter on the shelves. We recommend finding brands that are pure and have as few ingredients as possible.

Specialty ingredients—such as fancy pistachio or walnut oil, and peanut butter powder—are not ingredients we have the ability to make at home. We only use these types of ingredients modestly or offer alternatives, as we know they can be costly and harder to find.

STORING NUTS AND SEEDS

Due to their high oil content, nuts and seeds, especially those that have had their shells removed, should be kept in cold storage to prevent them from going rancid. If you plan on using them within a week or two, storing them in an airtight container in the refrigerator should be fine.

We recommend checking out the bulk bins to get better acquainted with all the varieties of nuts and seeds that interest you. Bulk bins offer a wonderful opportunity to purchase smaller quantities, with the added bonus that they're usually more affordable than their prepackaged counterparts.

If you like to buy in bulk, packing, labeling, and storing nuts and seeds in the freezer is best. Because the majority of the moisture in nuts comes from fat, nuts defrost quickly once removed from the freezer. Choose glass containers over plastic to store the goods, as the amount of oil in nuts can leach toxins from plastic containers.

SOAKING NUTS AND SEEDS

Nuts, seeds, and whole grains all naturally contain nutritional inhibitors, such as phytic acid and enzyme inhibitors. These compounds prevent germination from taking place until the right time and conditions are met. That's good for the plant, but not ideal for us because it also stops the good nutrients from being absorbed by our bodies. An efficient way to help eliminate these inhibitors and unlock the most nutrition out of such foods is to soak them in filtered water at room temperature for a few hours (see sidebar). This step will also soften the nuts for preparations that need to be completely smooth once blended, such as sauces or spreads. Soaking nuts is especially necessary for those of us who aren't the proud owners of fancy, and often costly, high-speed blenders.

The best way to prepare your nuts for soaking is to rinse raw, preferably organic, nuts under clear water in a fine-mesh sieve. Place the rinsed nuts and 1 teaspoon of salt in a glass bowl, glass measuring cup, or glass jar. Cover with warm filtered water in a 1:2 ratio, or 1 cup of nuts (weight will vary, but approximately 120 g) to 2 cups (470 ml) water. Just be sure the nuts or seeds are covered by an extra 2 inches (5 cm) of liquid.

Cover the container with a lid, plastic wrap, or cloth towel. Soak at room temperature. Soaking times will vary, but a good rule of thumb is that the denser the nut, the longer the soaking time. If you want to make it a bit more straightforward, aim for an average of 7 hours, or overnight, to soak most nuts. That's what we usually do.

Once ready, rinse and drain thoroughly. Use immediately in recipes where nuts or seeds need to be (or can be) moist, or store in an airtight container in the refrigerator for up to 5 days.

SOAKING TIME GUIDELINES

First, a quick reminder that nuts and seeds should be soaked at room temperature. The following soaking times are guidelines. It'll be fine if you go over a little bit, so don't fret. Just be sure to keep it relatively close, especially in warm weather. You don't want the nuts and seeds to get too bloated, or start smelling funky due to fermentation and turn sour.

Almonds: 8 to 12 hours

Brazil nuts: 2 to 4 hours

Cashews: 2 to 4 hours

Hazelnuts: 8 to 12 hours

Macadamia nuts: 2 hours

Pecans: 6 hours

Pine nuts: 4 hours

Pistachios: 4 hours

Pumpkin seeds: 6 hours

Sesame seeds, hulled: 6 hours

Sunflower seeds, hulled: 6 hours

Walnuts: 6 hours

In recipes that need soaked nuts or seeds to be dry, use an oven or dehydrator to bring them back to dry form. Note that using the oven will cancel the raw profile of the nuts, as raw foods cannot be heated above 104°F (40°C) to be considered as such. If using the oven, set it to the lowest temperature, line a baking sheet with parchment paper, and evenly place the soaked nuts or seeds on top. Drying times will vary, so be sure to check occasionally until the nuts or seeds are crunchy and not soft anymore. If using a dehydrator, we recommend following the manufacturer's instructions; it may take up to 24 hours for nuts or seeds to dry. Once the nuts or seeds are thoroughly dry—this is important to prevent mold growth—and cooled, you can store them in airtight containers at room temperature until ready to use.

Short on time? Ready to make that recipe, but forgot to soak your nuts? Some nuts can be boiled instead of soaked to achieve that softness to use in recipes (though this method doesn't necessarily carry the same nutritional benefits as a long soak). For example, cashews can be boiled for about 15 minutes, then rinsed and drained for use, just as if they had been soaked overnight. Another quick-soak method that is used strictly for softening, and has no nutritional benefit, is to place your nuts or seeds in a heat-safe bowl, cover with boiling water, let sit for about 10 minutes, drain, rinse, and use as directed in the recipe.

GLOSSARY

We strive to use readily available ingredients in all our recipes. Here's a quick rundown of a few that might be new or unknown to you. If you cannot locate some of the following ingredients at your local grocery store, international food store, or natural food store, don't forget to check online! Whenever available and affordable, choose organic ingredients over conventional ones.

Berbere spice: Berbere is an Ethiopian spice mix made with fenugreek, chile, and paprika. It has varying levels of heat depending on the brand. It's best to use it to taste. Berbere can be purchased at well-stocked markets and online, or can be homemade. There's a good recipe on www.epicurious.com, originally from *Gourmet*. Just search for "Ethiopian Spice Mix (Berbere)."

Chickpea flour: Also known as gram flour, garbanzo bean flour, and besan, this protein-rich flour is made from ground chickpeas. It is quite bitter in raw form, so wait until the preparation is cooked before having a taste. Garbanzo fava bean flour (a blend of chickpea and fava bean flours) can be used instead of chickpea flour. Indian grocers are a great place to find the flour, and often for really affordable prices.

Fire-roasted diced tomatoes: These flavorful canned tomatoes are used in a few of our dishes, but we know they can be hard to find depending on where you live. Tester and friend Liz Wyman replaces them with regular diced tomatoes and adds a few drops of liquid smoke to make up for the lack of roasted flavor.

Harissa spice: This spicy North African flavoring is made from a blend of hot peppers and other spices. It comes in a paste or dry blend. You can use either form in equal amounts, to taste. Harissa can be found in the ethnic aisle of well-stocked grocery stores or online.

Kala namak: Also known as black salt, this pinkish colored salt is pungent with sulfur, which gives an egg-like flavor to foods. It can be found in most specialty and spice shops, and it can be easily found online. A little goes a long way, so be wise when sprinkling.

Nutritional yeast: Lovingly referred to by vegans around the world as "nooch," this flaky yellow yeast is usually grown on molasses. It has a nutty, rich, almost cheesy flavor that also adds a nutritional boost to your foods (Hello, B vitamins!). Be sure to seek out "vegetarian support" formulas. You can find nutritional yeast in the vitamin and supplement section of most health food stores.

Pomegranate molasses: Pomegranate molasses, made by boiling down the juice of tart pomegranates, is used primarily in Mediterranean cooking. It can be found in international grocery stores or online. We recommend the recipe found on simplyrecipes.com. That's the one we used to make the recipes in this book, preparing it with ¼ cup (80 g) agave nectar instead of sugar. The lemon juice used in this particular recipe helps the pomegranate juice retain its beautiful color once turned into molasses.

Salt: For the most part, we prefer telling you to use salt "to taste" instead of giving a set amount. Just remember it's easier to add extra salt than it is to remove it! We use both coarse kosher salt and fine sea salt. If you don't have coarse kosher salt, use half the amount of fine sea salt wherever kosher salt is called for.

Sriracha: Made from chile peppers, garlic, vinegar, and salt ground together to form a smooth paste, this hot sauce is addictive. Be sure to check the ingredients because some brands contain fish sauce.

Sumac: We've grown extremely fond of this ground Middle Eastern berry that imparts food with a tart, lemony, and subtly salty flavor. Sumac can be purchased at Middle Eastern markets and at online stores, such as Penzeys and KhanaPakana.

Tamari: Tamari is a richly flavored, Japanese-style soy sauce. We prefer gluten-free reduced-sodium tamari. If you cannot find tamari, use reduced-sodium soy sauce in its place. (The Gluten-Free Potential label won't apply anymore if gluten-free tamari is replaced with soy sauce.)

Vegan milks: Two of our favorites are the unsweetened, plain, almond milk and the almond-coconut blend. You can use whatever you prefer, just remember to go with unsweetened plain vegan milk for savory applications.

Whole wheat pastry flour: This flour is ground from soft white wheat berries. If it isn't available, you can use an equal combination of whole wheat flour and all-purpose flour, or only all-purpose flour instead.

Za'atar blend: Za'atar is a generic name for a mix of Middle Eastern herbs and spices used in Arab cuisine. Different regions have different varieties of the mix. Usually it is a blend of thyme, oregano, and marjoram mixed with toasted sesame seeds, salt, and other spices. Za'atar blends often include sumac. We love the bonappetit.com recipe for homemade za'atar, created by Chef Silvena Rowe. If time permits, use toasted sesame seeds to add even more oomph to this particular mix.

RECIPE LABELS

Many of the recipes contained in this cookbook have one or more of the following labels:

▶ GLUTEN-FREE POTENTIAL

Recipes that can be safe to enjoy by those who need to eat gluten-free foods. Make sure to thoroughly check ingredients for safe use and purchase ingredients that are certified gluten-free. Contact the ingredient manufacturer, if needed, for up-to-date information.

▶ SOY-FREE POTENTIAL

Recipes that are free of any soy products, provided soymilk isn't used wherever vegan milk is called for. Please thoroughly check labels and contact the manufacturer, if needed. Be sure to check unexpected ingredients, such as vegetable broth and nut milks, as they may contain hidden soy. If using nonstick cooking spray, remember to check for soy lecithin, too. If you cannot find soy-free nonstick cooking spray, pour your favorite neutral-flavored oil in a food-safe spray bottle for moderated greasing instead. Or even more simply, lightly apply the oil with a brush wherever it's needed.

▶ OIL-FREE POTENTIAL

Recipes that can be made without the use of extracted oils. These recipes will not necessarily be low in fat as they may contain naturally high-in-fat foods, such as nuts, avocados, and coconut. Some of these recipes will be naturally oil-free, while others will offer alternative methods of preparation to be made oil-free.

▶ QUICK AND EASY

Recipes that take less than 30 minutes to whip up, provided you have intermediate cooking or baking skills.

2

NUTS AND SEEDS BASICS

Getting Started with Nut- and Seed-Based Staples, Spreads, and Sauces

Just perusing the aisles at any grocery store will provide you with many options for nut butters and milks. Even nut-based ice creams, coffee creamers, and cheeses have made their way onto the shelves of mainstream markets. While we often reach for these premade items simply out of convenience, we also pride ourselves on being able to make all of these staples from scratch in our very own kitchens. Because of the popularity of plant-based diet, an awakening of the foodie spirit, and a return to the slow-food mentality all over the world, we thought it important to share these techniques with you, without further ado.

Roasting Nuts or Seeds

▶ **NUT OR SEED**: ANY ▶ GLUTEN-FREE POTENTIAL ▶ OIL-FREE ▶ QUICK AND EASY
▶ SOY-FREE POTENTIAL

Toasting nuts and seeds brings out their incredible flavors, but did you know that this step also helps reduce phytic acids? Granted, it is to a lesser extent than what soaking does (page 14), but toasting still makes the nuts and seeds more digestible than when left raw. While it's possible to purchase most unsalted nuts or seeds in dry-roasted form at the store, you might want to be completely hands-on and DIY, freshly toasting only what you need and keeping the rest raw for other purposes.

1 to 2 cups (weight will vary, about 120 to 240 g) raw nuts or seeds of choice

Recipe Note

The words "toasted" and "roasted" are used interchangeably by many manufacturers and cookbook authors. Roasting usually means placing food in a dry heat source in order to cook it through. Toasting means adding color and extra flavor to food. While they're technically not the same process, and "toasted" would be more accurate, you'll see us use them interchangeably in this nut-centric book, too.

Preheat the oven to 300°F (150°C, or gas mark 2).

Place the nuts or larger seeds in a single layer on a small, rimmed baking sheet. Bake on the middle rack until golden brown and fragrant. Keep a very close eye on the nuts or seeds so that they don't burn. We prefer checking every 5 minutes or so, stirring to make sure the nuts or seeds brown evenly. Walnuts, pecans, pistachios, and most seeds take about 8 minutes to toast. Most other nuts take about 15 minutes. Nuts with skins, such as hazelnuts or walnuts, can be wrapped and rubbed in a clean towel, or between fingers once sufficiently cooled, to remove as much of the skin as possible.

Smaller seeds, such as sesame, should be toasted in a heavy-bottomed, dry skillet over moderate heat. Stir them frequently until fragrant.

YIELD: 1 to 2 cups (weight will vary, about 120 to 240 g) toasted nuts or seeds of choice

Basic Nut or Seed Butters

▶ **NUT OR SEED**: ANY ▶ GLUTEN-FREE POTENTIAL ▶ OIL-FREE ▶ QUICK AND EASY
▶ SOY-FREE POTENTIAL

Sure, grabbing a jar of ready-made, natural nut or seed butter is a breeze, but the cost can give you a major headache when you get to the checkout line. We're looking at you, Mister Hazelnut Butter. The good news is it only takes a few steps to make your very own butter from the nuts or seeds you love the most, quite often at a fraction of the price. Don't be afraid to mix and match to your heart's content: a favorite combination of ours is crunchy, roasted peanut butter, flax, and chia seeds.

2 cups (weight will vary, about 240 g) raw nuts or seeds of choice

Generous pinch or two of fine sea salt

Neutral-flavored oil, as needed (not all nuts will need this, but cashews and almonds usually do)

If you use roasted nuts or seeds, see the instructions on page 20. Remove from the oven, let cool a few minutes, and transfer to a food processor with salt, if desired.

If using raw nuts or seeds, transfer directly to a food processor along with the salt, if desired.

Process until the nuts or seeds release their oil, making for a spreadable nut butter. The processing time will vary, depending on the nuts or seeds, and machine. The harder the nut (almonds, for example), the longer. The softer the nut (peanuts), the shorter.

Stop the machine occasionally to scrape the sides with a rubber spatula. If the motor starts to overheat, power off to let it cool before continuing. If the nuts or seeds have a hard time transforming into butter, drizzle neutral-flavored vegetable oil as needed while the machine runs. For crunchy-style butter, add a handful of nuts to the butter when it looks ready to be jarred. Pulse until coarse, or until you reach the desired level of crunchiness.

Store in an airtight jar in the refrigerator for up to 2 weeks. Note that the oil will separate. Leave the jar at room temperature for a little while, then stir the oil in with a knife and some elbow grease. If you're looking for extra nutrition and easier digestibility, try using activated and thoroughly dehydrated nuts or seeds (page 14).

YIELD: About 1 cup (weight will vary, about 240 g) nut or seed butter

Basic Nut or Seed Milks

▶ NUT OR SEED: ANY ▶ GLUTEN-FREE POTENTIAL ▶ OIL-FREE ▶ SOY-FREE POTENTIAL

We've already confessed to reaching for store-bought vegan milks for convenience, but we also love the process of making our own nut milks at home when time and energy permit. There's just something about preparing your food with your own two hands, knowing exactly what goes into it. Our personal favorite nut milks are plain cashew or almond. We look forward to you discovering your favorite, if you haven't already!

1 cup (weight will vary, about 120 g) raw nuts or seeds of choice

6 to 6½ cups (1.4 to 1.5 L) filtered water, divided

Pinch fine sea salt

1 Medjool date or other moist date, pitted and chopped, to taste (optional)

Pure vanilla extract, to taste (optional)

Recipe Note

To make plant-based creamer, we find cashews to be the softest and most efficient candidates. Simply add 1¼ cups (295 ml) water and a pinch of salt after soaking and rinsing the cashews. For a richer-tasting creamer, add ¼ cup (60 ml) full-fat coconut milk after squeezing the milk through the nut milk bag. Use a blender to combine. Store in an airtight jar in the refrigerator for up to 1 week. Shake before use. Yields about 2 cups (470 ml).

Place the nuts or seeds in a medium bowl or 4-cup (940 ml) glass measuring cup. Cover with 2 cups (470 ml) water. Cover with plastic wrap or a lid, and let stand at room temperature. Follow the guidelines on page 15 to find out the soaking time. Drain the nuts or seeds in a fine-mesh sieve, and give them a quick rinse. Discard the soaking water.

To make plain milk: In a blender, combine the nuts or seeds with 2 to 2½ cups (470 to 590 ml) fresh water. The quantity depends on how thick you want the milk. Add a pinch of salt. Blend until the nuts or seeds are pulverized. Jump to the filtering instructions.

To make lightly flavored milk: Combine the nuts or seeds, 2 to 2½ cups (470 to 590 ml) water, salt, date, and vanilla in a blender. Blend until the nuts or seeds are pulverized.

To filter: Place a fine-mesh sieve lined with an open nut milk bag on top of a large glass measuring cup, and slowly pour the milk into the bag. Filter the milk by carefully squeezing the bag, allowing the milk to pass through while keeping the pulp behind in the bag. Store the pulp in an airtight container for up to 4 days or freeze it for up to 3 months. Add it to your morning oatmeal, bread, and even veggie burgers (if the pulp comes from unflavored milk).

Store the milk in an airtight bottle for up to 5 days. Shake well before use.

YIELD: 2 to 2½ cups (470 to 590 ml) milk

Basic Nut or Seed Flours

▶ **NUT OR SEED**: ANY ▶ GLUTEN-FREE POTENTIAL ▶ OIL-FREE ▶ QUICK AND EASY
▶ SOY-FREE POTENTIAL

You might find yourself wondering if there is a difference between nut meals and nut flours. It turns out that nut meals are usually slightly coarser than nut flours. Nuts also don't need to have their skin removed in order to qualify as a meal, whereas nut flours usually are blanched and ground quite finely. Note that these appellations are used interchangeably by some manufacturers. Most recipes won't suffer one bit if meals and flours are used interchangeably, but it can be a bit trickier in macarons and light cakes where finely ground flours should be used. We will mention whenever such a difference matters in our recipes.

Also note that delicious, protein-rich peanut flour or powder—such as Protein Plus or Bell Plantation's PB2—cannot be perfectly replicated at home. The commercial kind is fully or partly defatted for lower-calorie, finer results.

1 cup (weight will vary, about 120 g) raw nuts or seeds of choice

For best results, nuts or seeds must be at room temperature before being placed in the food processor, grinder, high-speed blender, etc. Pulse, then blend or process until a fine flour is obtained. Do not overprocess! You're looking for flour, not nut or seed butter. The longer the machine turns, the more the blades and motor heat up, and the more likely it is the outcome will turn into a paste.

For the finest results, pass the resulting flour through a fine-mesh sieve. Place the coarser bits back into the machine and grind again, or use them in oatmeal or wherever using a coarser flour is not an issue.

Note that it's best to grind-as-you-go rather than preparing a lot of flour at one time, for the freshest results. This is especially the case with flax.

For smaller amounts, consider using a mini food processor, coffee grinder, or spice grinder. If you're looking for extra nutrition and easier digestibility, try using activated and thoroughly dehydrated nuts or seeds (page 14).

YIELD: Approximately 1 cup (120 g)

Almond-Milk Cream Cheese Spread

▶ **NUT AND SEED**: ALMOND AND CHIA ▶ SOY-FREE POTENTIAL ▶ GLUTEN-FREE POTENTIAL

This creamy spread can be used on toast, bagels, or crackers. The recipe below is for a plain spread, but feel free to experiment with different flavors. We have listed several add-ins that we like in the Recipe Note below.

1 cup (108 g) dry slivered almonds
(or whole skinned almonds)

½ cup (120 ml) unsweetened
almond milk

2 tablespoons (28 g) refined
coconut oil (unrefined will work,
but leaves a coconut flavor)

1 tablespoon (15 ml) apple cider vinegar

1 tablespoon (7 g) finely ground
chia seeds

1 tablespoon (12 g) raw sugar

¼ teaspoon salt

Bring a pot of water to a boil. Add the almonds, and boil for 20 minutes, or until tender. Strain, rinse, and drain of excess water. Add the boiled almonds and all the other ingredients to a high-speed blender. Purée until smooth. Transfer to an airtight dish and place in the refrigerator for a few hours to set before using.

YIELD: 10 ounces (283 g)

Recipe Note

To flavor your spread, try stirring in the following after it has set: fruit preserves; garlic and chives; cinnamon and brown sugar; taco seasoning; dill and parsley. The possibilities really are endless.

Simple Almond or Cashew Spread

▶ **NUT**: ALMOND OR CASHEW ▶ GLUTEN-FREE POTENTIAL ▶ OIL-FREE

Making this kind of tangy spread is a bit time-consuming, but it is a worthwhile endeavor as the results are quite delicious and versatile. Use the spread as a replacement for cream cheese in both savory and sweet applications. We love it with briny flavors, like tapenade. It can also be used as a filling with fruity spreads or jams in stuffed French toast!

Note that if your food processor has a capacity of more than 6 to 7 cups (1.4 to 1.7 L), it's wise to double the recipe to get the smoothest results. Otherwise, your machine will struggle a bit to do its crushing and blending job.

1 cup (145 g) skinned almonds or 1 cup (140 g) raw cashews, soaked overnight (page 14)

¼ cup (60 g) unsweetened plain vegan yogurt or chilled coconut cream (from the top of an unshaken refrigerated can)

1 to 1½ tablespoons (15 to 23 ml) fresh lemon juice (the more, the tangier)

½ teaspoon coarse kosher salt

¼ cup (60 ml) water, as needed

Combine all the ingredients, except the water, in a high-speed blender or food processor. Process until completely smooth. Add the water, 1 tablespoon (15 ml) at a time, if needed. The timing will depend on the power of the machine you use. Stop to scrape the sides occasionally. Transfer to a glass container, and cover tightly with a lid or plastic wrap.

Leave at room temperature for 6 hours or up to 24 hours, until the preparation smells tangy and looks "cracked" on the surface. The timing will depend on the temperature: The warmer it is, the shorter it will take. If using a measuring cup with markings, you will notice that the preparation will have expanded from approximately 1½ cups (355 ml) to 1¾ cups (415 ml).

Transfer to the refrigerator. Chill for 24 hours or more before use, to let the flavor develop. The spread can be stored airtight in the refrigerator for up to 2 weeks after that.

YIELD: 1¾ cups (320 g)

Simple Almond or Cashew Sour Cream

▶ **NUT**: ALMOND OR CASHEW
▶ GLUTEN-FREE POTENTIAL ▶ OIL-FREE
▶ SOY-FREE POTENTIAL

Put this sour cream to great use in our Loaded Potatoes (page 80) and anywhere regular sour cream usually comes into play. Granted, it takes more time than just grabbing a tub of vegan sour cream at the store, but look at the benefits: only 4 ingredients, soy-free potential (if you're not using soy yogurt in the spread), and very little hands-on work overall.

½ cup (92 g) Simple Almond or Cashew Spread (page 26)

¼ cup (60 ml) unsweetened plain almond or cashew milk

1 teaspoon white balsamic vinegar

Salt (a few pinches, you can always add more later)

Combine all the ingredients in a small bowl, and whisk thoroughly. Cover tightly and leave in the refrigerator for 24 hours or more before use, to let the flavor develop.

YIELD: ¾ cup (140 g)

Simple Cashew Mayo

▶ **NUT**: CASHEW ▶ SOY-FREE
POTENTIAL ▶ GLUTEN-FREE
POTENTIAL ▶ QUICK AND EASY

This mayo is rich with a slight nutty undertone. Use it as you would any mayo!

2 cups (224 g) cashews, soaked overnight or boiled for 15 minutes (page 14)

1 cup (235 ml) canola or other mild-flavored vegetable oil

½ cup (120 ml) unsweetened plain nut milk

1 tablespoon (10 g) dry ground mustard seed

2 teaspoons (10 ml) fresh lemon juice

1 teaspoon apple cider vinegar

1 teaspoon agave nectar

1 teaspoon salt

¼ teaspoon black salt (kala namak) (optional)

Add all the ingredients to a blender and purée until silky smooth. Thin with additional milk to desired consistency. Store in an airtight container in the refrigerator for up to 2 weeks.

YIELD: 2½ cups (560 g)

Peanut Chipotle Ranch Dressing

▶ **NUT**: PEANUT ▶ QUICK AND EASY ▶ OIL-FREE POTENTIAL ▶ GLUTEN-FREE POTENTIAL

Making your own sauces and dressings can breathe new life into the typical green salad, and this dressing is no exception. Spicy from the chipotle, yet cool and creamy, because ranch!

1 block (16 ounces, or 454 g) silken tofu

2 tablespoons (32 g) peanut butter

1 chipotle in adobo sauce

2 teaspoons (10 ml) of adobo sauce

2 teaspoons (1 g) dried parsley

1 teaspoon dried dill (or 1 tablespoon [3 g] fresh)

1 teaspoon minced garlic

¼ teaspoon black pepper

Salt (optional)

Add all the ingredients to a blender and purée until smooth. Refrigerate in an airtight container for up to 2 weeks.

YIELD: 1½ cups (455 ml)

Tahini Sumac Dressing

▶ **SEED**: SESAME (TAHINI) ▶ QUICK AND EASY ▶ GLUTEN-FREE POTENTIAL ▶ SOY-FREE POTENTIAL

If we could get away with pouring this rich and tart dressing straight into our gullets, we probably would. It's perfect to coat virtually any salad, of course (page 145). It's also great as a dip for protein-centric meals such as falafel or vegan burgers, as well as drizzled over baked potatoes or steamed vegetables.

¼ cup (64 g) roasted tahini paste

¼ cup (60 ml) water

2 tablespoons (30 ml) grapeseed oil (or other neutral-flavored oil)

2 tablespoons (30 ml) seasoned rice vinegar

2 teaspoons (5 g) ground sumac, to taste

½ teaspoon coarse kosher salt

1 large clove garlic, chopped

1 teaspoon agave nectar or brown rice syrup

Combine all the ingredients in a small blender, or place in a glass measuring cup and use an immersion blender. Blend until perfectly smooth. Use immediately, and store leftovers in an airtight container in the refrigerator for up to 4 days. Shake or stir before use. The dressing is likely to thicken after refrigeration: You can stir 1 tablespoon (15 ml) of water into each 2 tablespoons (30 ml) of the dressing to thin it out again. It won't lose anything on the flavor front.

YIELD: ¾ cup (180 ml) dressing

Creamy Sunflower Buffalo Sauce

▶ **SEED**: SUNFLOWER ▶ QUICK AND EASY ▶ SOY-FREE POTENTIAL

This easy blender sauce works well as a dip for veggies, salad dressing, pizza sauce, on nachos (!!!), and as the base for the Buffalo Coleslaw (page 140).

1 cup (128 g) sunflower kernels, soaked at least 6 hours or simmered 15 to 20 minutes, rinsed and drained

¾ cup (180 ml) unsweetened nut milk

½ cup (120 ml) mild-flavored vegetable oil

⅓ cup (80 ml) of your favorite hot sauce (Red Rooster or Frank's work well)

2 tablespoons (20 g) minced garlic

1 tablespoon (8 g) onion powder

1 teaspoon Dijon mustard

¼ teaspoon salt, to taste

Add all the ingredients to a blender and purée until silky smooth. If you have a high-powered blender, this will be no problem. If you have a less-than-stellar blender, but you also happen to have an immersion blender, opt for the latter as it whips the sauce into silky goodness quite nicely.

Store in an airtight container in the refrigerator until ready to use.

YIELD: 2½ cups (590 ml)

Thai Peanut Sauce

▶ **NUT**: PEANUT ▶ QUICK AND EASY ▶ GLUTEN-FREE POTENTIAL

Nothing revolutionary here, but we would be remiss if we didn't include this sauce, and at least one recipe using it (page 110), in a book about nuts. We know, we know, peanuts are legumes!

¾ cup (192 g) creamy, no-stir peanut butter

¾ cup (180 ml) water (add more or less to thicken your sauce to drizzle-able consistency)

¼ cup (120 ml) tamari

¼ cup (60 ml) sesame oil (not toasted)

¼ cup (60 ml) agave nectar

1 inch (2.5 cm) fresh ginger, peeled and chopped

¼ to 1 teaspoon red chili flakes, to taste (optional)

Add all the ingredients to a blender and blend until smooth. Store in an airtight container in the refrigerator for up to 2 weeks.

YIELD: Just over 2 cups (485 ml)

Cheesy Almond Gravy

▶ **NUT**: ALMOND ▶ SOY-FREE POTENTIAL ▶ QUICK AND EASY

Mmmm. Gravy. Rich and savory and salty and creamy and . . . well, you get the picture. This gravy is inspired by the fine folks that decided to pour gravy all over french fries and then top it with cheese curds. Otherwise known as an amazing dish called poutine. This almond gravy puts the cheesiness right in the sauce, and the little almond bits are reminiscent of little bits of cheese. It works well with all sorts of dishes. Pour it over mashed potatoes, roasted cauliflower, brown rice, sautéed greens, and of course french fries!

2 tablespoons (30 ml) vegetable oil

1 tablespoon (10 g) minced garlic

¼ cup (30 g) whole wheat pastry flour

1 cup (235 ml) unsweetened almond milk

1 cup (235 ml) vegetable broth

1 cup (96 g) almond meal

¼ cup (30 g) nutritional yeast

½ teaspoon black pepper, to taste

1 tablespoon (18 g) yellow miso

Heat the oil over medium-high heat. Add in the garlic and sauté for 2 to 3 minutes, until fragrant. Whisk in the flour. Continue to cook and stir until a golden paste forms, about 2 to 3 minutes.

Slowly whisk in the almond milk, broth, almond meal, nutritional yeast, and pepper. Continue to cook and stir until thickened and no lumps remain, about 5 to 7 minutes. (If you prefer a silky smooth gravy, we recommend blending with an immersion blender, or carefully transferring to a blender and blending until desired consistency is reached.)

Remove from the heat and stir in the miso. Serve immediately, or store in an airtight container in the refrigerator for up to a week.

YIELD: 2½ cups (590 ml)

Pistachio or Pepita Radish Guacamole

▶ **NUT OR SEED**: PISTACHIO OR PEPITA ▶ GLUTEN-FREE POTENTIAL ▶ OIL-FREE ▶ QUICK AND EASY ▶ SOY-FREE POTENTIAL

Guacamole connoisseurs-slash-testers for this book declared that this might well be "the best guacamole" they'd ever had. Hooray!

1 ripe-but-firm Haas avocado, halved, pitted, and peeled, quartered

2 large or 4 small trimmed red radishes, quartered

½ seeded jalapeño pepper, to taste

Salt

2 small scallions (white and green parts), coarsely chopped

¼ cup (4 g) fresh cilantro leaves

2 teaspoons to 1 tablespoon (10 to 15 ml) fresh lime juice, to taste

1 clove garlic, minced

3 tablespoons (23 g) roasted pistachios or pepitas

Place all the ingredients in a food processor, and pulse to combine until slightly chunky. Alternatively, mash the avocados by hand, grate or press the garlic, and mince all other ingredients by hand. Serve immediately as a sandwich spread, dip for chips, wherever you like to use your guac', or cover tightly for up to 1 hour in the refrigerator. We've kept the yield on the moderate side to prevent oxidation, but you can double the recipe if you know it will get eaten the same day.

YIELD: 1 packed cup (260 g)

Cashew Radish Dip

▶ **NUT**: CASHEW ▶ GLUTEN-FREE POTENTIAL ▶ OIL-FREE ▶ QUICK AND EASY ▶ SOY-FREE POTENTIAL

A super simple, refreshing, pinkish dip for those sweltering summer nights when a hot stove and you are temporary sworn enemies.

¾ cup (180 g) Simple Cashew Spread (page 26)

4 ounces (113 g) red radishes, chopped

1 small scallion, white and green parts (2 tablespoons, or 10 g chopped)

1 tablespoon (15 ml) fresh lemon juice

1 teaspoon dried dill or 2 teaspoons to 1 tablespoon (2 to 3 g) fresh

½ teaspoon coarse kosher salt, to taste

Place all the ingredients in a food processor. Pulse to combine, stopping to scrape the sides with a rubber spatula once or twice. Leave slightly chunky.

Refrigerate in an airtight container for at least 1 hour before serving. Serve as a veggie dip, topping for baked potatoes, or as a sandwich spread. Or use it on toast or whole-grain crackers, topped with razor-thin cucumber slices for a refreshing snack. Store leftovers in an airtight container for up to 3 days.

YIELD: 1 cup (330 g)

Citrusy Cashew Baba Ghanoush

▶ **NUT**: CASHEW ▶ GLUTEN-FREE POTENTIAL ▶ OIL-FREE ▶ SOY-FREE POTENTIAL

Baba ghanoush is usually made with tahini (sesame paste). We put a new spin on it by using roasted cashew butter instead, paired with refreshing citrusy notes. Added bonus of this use of eggplant? People who strongly dislike the texture of the purple-coated veggie—but not its flavor—will happily partake!

1 medium (17 ounces, or 482 g) eggplant, left whole and poked a few times with a fork

1 to 2 tablespoons (15 to 30 ml) fresh lemon juice, to taste

3 tablespoons (48 g) roasted cashew butter

1½ teaspoons ground sumac

½ teaspoon harissa (paste or dry blend), to taste

1 clove garlic, grated or pressed

Generous ¼ teaspoon fine sea salt, to taste

¼ cup (4 g) fresh cilantro leaves

3 tablespoons (15 g) chopped scallion

Pomegranate molasses (page 17), for garnish (optional)

Place the eggplant on a baking sheet or dish. Broil the eggplant until tender, about 25 minutes. Turn it every 10 minutes to prevent burning. Let cool slightly before handling. Trim the end and peel the eggplant. Discard the seeds if there are any.

Transfer to a food processor. Add 1 tablespoon (15 ml) of lemon juice, cashew butter, sumac, harissa, garlic, salt, and cilantro. Pulse to blend and combine. Add the scallion and combine. It's okay if the mixture remains slightly chunky. Add extra lemon juice after tasting, if desired. Adjust the seasoning as well. Serve immediately with a drizzle of pomegranate molasses, and toasted pita bread or pita chips, or use as a sandwich spread.

YIELD: 1½ cups (390 g) baba ghanoush

Pistachio Dukkah

▶ NUT AND SEED: PISTACHIO AND SESAME ▶ GLUTEN-FREE POTENTIAL ▶ OIL-FREE
▶ SOY-FREE POTENTIAL ▶ QUICK AND EASY

Dukkah is an Egyptian condiment composed of a variety of nuts, spices, and herbs: pretty much anything goes! We made ours super-colorful by using green-hued pistachios and yellow turmeric. It's pictured here with our Pine Nut Parm-y Sprinkles (page 36). So handsome you almost don't want to eat it (almost). We love sprinkling it over Cashew Avocado Toast (page 104), but you can use it as a salad topper, in sandwiches, on top of whole-grain salads, as a bread dip. It's also great as a popcorn topper, just be sure to make a finer mixture so that it sticks to the popped corn better.

2 tablespoons (15 g) shelled, toasted pistachios, coarsely chopped

1 tablespoon (7 g) toasted ivory, brown, or black sesame seeds

½ to ¾ teaspoon ground coriander, to taste

½ to ¾ teaspoon ground cumin, to taste

½ teaspoon red pepper flakes

½ teaspoon ground sumac

¼ teaspoon coarse kosher salt, to taste

¼ teaspoon ground turmeric

Place all the ingredients in a mortar. Slowly crush with the pestle until you reach the desired grind: We like ours a bit coarse to keep some crunch. You just don't want to turn it into a paste. Alternatively, you can also use a spice grinder. Simply pulse a few times until the desired grind is reached.

Serve as you wish. Leftovers of dukkah can be stored in an airtight container at room temperature or in the refrigerator for up to 2 weeks, for optimal freshness.

YIELD: ⅓ cup (40 g) dukkah

Recipe Notes

• Feel free to double the recipe if you know you will use a lot of dukkah. We prefer going for a smaller batch so that it's at its freshest with each use. It's also easier to crush with a smaller quantity if your mortar (or spice grinder) is on the small side, to avoid spilling.

• If you have whole coriander and cumin seeds that you can freshly toast and grind, that's even better! Note that it takes approximately 1 teaspoon whole coriander or cumin seeds to make ½ teaspoon ground, or 1½ teaspoons whole for ¾ teaspoon ground.

Pine Nut Parm-y Sprinkles Two Ways

▶ **NUT**: PINE NUT ▶ OIL-FREE POTENTIAL ▶ SOY-FREE POTENTIAL
▶ GLUTEN-FREE POTENTIAL ▶ QUICK AND EASY

Move over grated Parmesan! There's a new, cruelty-free gal in town, and she's ready to knock your pasta, salads, and avocado toast into next Tuesday! (You can see both sprinkles variations in the wooden spoons alongside the Pistachio Dukkah on page 34.)

FOR THE PESTO PINE NUT PARM-Y SPRINKLES:

2 tablespoons (15 g) raw or toasted pine nuts

2 tablespoons (15 g) nutritional yeast

2 teaspoons (1 g) dried basil

1 teaspoon lemon pepper

1 teaspoon garlic powder

1 teaspoon salt

FOR THE SMOKED CHIPOTLE PINE NUT PARM-Y SPRINKLES:

2 tablespoons (15 g) raw or toasted pine nuts

2 tablespoons (15 g) nutritional yeast

1 tablespoon (18 g) smoked salt

2 teaspoons (6 g) garlic powder

1 teaspoon onion powder

½ teaspoon chipotle powder

½ teaspoon paprika

Add all the ingredients to a spice grinder, clean coffee grinder, or very dry high-speed blender. Pulse until a very fine powder forms. Store in an airtight container in the refrigerator indefinitely. When ready to use, give the container a good shake to loosen up the sprinkles.

YIELD: 6 tablespoons (48 g) Pesto and ½ cup (64 g) Smoked Chipotle

Pepita Pepper Hummus

▶ **SEED**: PEPITA ▶ GLUTEN-FREE POTENTIAL ▶ OIL-FREE ▶ SOY-FREE POTENTIAL

A tahini-free hummus? Say it isn't so! Actually yes, it is. It also happens to be oil-free, but who's counting? Roasted pepitas, also known as hulled pumpkin seeds, are a great, innovative flavor stand-in for sesame seed–paste. For the roasted peppers and za'atar blend, see our pointers in Sesame Za'atar Pepper Soup (page 116).

½ roasted poblano pepper, peeled, cored, and seeded

½ roasted green bell pepper, peeled, cored, and seeded

½ roasted jalapeño pepper, peeled, cored, and seeded

½ cup (60 g) roasted pepitas

½ cup (8 g) loose fresh cilantro leaves

1 clove garlic, grated or pressed

¼ cup plus 2 tablespoons (30 g) coarsely chopped scallion

1½ cups (256 g) cooked chickpeas

¾ teaspoon coarse kosher salt

½ teaspoon ground cumin

½ teaspoon ground coriander

1 tablespoon (15 ml) fresh lime juice

Lime wedges

Za'atar blend (page 17)

Combine all the ingredients, except the lime wedges and za'atar, in a food processor. Blend until mostly smooth. Stop occasionally to scrape the sides with a rubber spatula.

Transfer to an airtight container. Chill covered for at least 1 hour before serving.

Serve with pita chips or on toasted bread, with a few drops of juice squeezed from a lime wedge, and sprinkled with a pinch of za'atar.

YIELD: 2 cups (460 g)

Cashew Romesco Dip

▶ NUT: CASHEW ▶ GLUTEN-FREE POTENTIAL ▶ SOY-FREE POTENTIAL

We love to serve this flavorful red dip with crispy whole-grain crackers and veggie sticks, or even as a sandwich spread on crusty bread.

2 red bell peppers, halved and seeded

2 large cloves garlic, peeled and left whole

½ cup (70 g) roasted cashews

1 tablespoon (15 ml) extra-virgin olive oil or grapeseed oil

1 tablespoon (15 ml) white balsamic vinegar

½ teaspoon smoked paprika

½ teaspoon ground sumac

Salt and pepper

Preheat the oven to 450°F (230°C, or gas mark 8). Place the bell pepper halves and garlic on a baking sheet. Roast until blackened, about 30 minutes. Keep an eye on the peppers to prevent burning, and flip the garlic, removing it sooner if needed. Once ready, remove from the oven and place in a large bowl with a lid to steam for 10 minutes. Drain and peel the skin.

Place the peppers, garlic, and cashews in a food processor. Blend until mostly smooth. Add the oil, vinegar, paprika, and sumac. Blend until thoroughly combined and mostly smooth. Stop occasionally to scrape the sides of the machine with a rubber spatula. Add salt and pepper to taste, blending again to combine. Transfer to an airtight container and store in the refrigerator for at least 2 hours before serving, or overnight. Leftovers can be served for up to 4 days.

YIELD: 1 cup (270 g)

Clockwise from right: Cashew Radish Dip (page 32), Cashew Romesco Dip (this page), and Pepita Pepper Hummus (page 37).

Simple Nutty Cheese

▶ **NUT**: CASHEW

Making your own nut cheeses is such a gratifying experience. There are so many recipes available these days, which is pretty exciting! This is a very basic recipe. Beginner's vegan cheese, if you will. It requires no aging so you can get to your cheesy goodness within an hour or so. It is worthy of crackers and wine, or sliced on a sandwich. Try different add-ins and variations to suit your tastes.

Nonstick cooking spray

2 cups (470 ml) almond or cashew milk

¼ cup (10 g) agar flakes

1 cup (79 g) cashews, soaked at least 4 hours or simmered 15 to 20 minutes, rinsed and drained

¼ cup (60 g) nutritional yeast

2 tablespoons (36 g) yellow miso

2 tablespoons (30 ml) soy sauce or tamari

2 tablespoons (30 ml) refined coconut oil

1 tablespoon (8 g) onion powder

1 tablespoon (6 g) garlic powder

1 tablespoon (6 g) ground mustard

Have a loaf pan sprayed with nonstick cooking spray ready. Add the milk and the agar to a sauce pot, and bring to a boil. Meanwhile, place all the other ingredients into a blender and purée until smooth. If you are using optional add-ins (see Recipe Note), you can stir them in after puréeing to allow them to remain chunky and add depth and dimension to your cheese.

After the milk and agar have come to a full boil, keep the boil rolling for 3 to 5 minutes, until the agar is completely and fully dissolved. Add the blended mixture and stir vigorously. Remove from the heat and immediately pour into the loaf pan. Refrigerate for a few hours, or until hardened, before using.

YIELD: 1 loaf

Recipe Note

Optional add-ins! Try stirring in these favorites just after blending, and before adding to the agar mixture: liquid smoke, coarsely ground black pepper, red pepper flakes, fresh chopped herbs, minced garlic, caramelized onion, lavender petals, sun-dried tomatoes, truffle oil, or whatever you can dream up!

Tangy Almond Herbed Cheese Log

▶ **NUTS**: ALMOND AND CASHEW ▶ SOY-FREE POTENTIAL ▶ GLUTEN-FREE POTENTIAL

Soft, spreadable, and worthy of any cheese plate. This rich and tangy log spreads lovingly on crackers, sandwiches, bagels, avocado toast, and veggies.

8 ounces (22 g) raw cashews

3 ounces (85 g) unsweetened plain vegan yogurt

2 tablespoons (15 g) nutritional yeast

2 tablespoons (20 g) chia seeds, ground into a powder

1 tablespoon (18 g) white or yellow miso

1 tablespoons (15 ml) neutral-flavored oil

1 teaspoon (5 ml) fresh lemon juice

¼ teaspoon salt

⅛ teaspoon black pepper

1 teaspoon dried parsley

1 teaspoon dried tarragon

½ teaspoon dried dill

¼ teaspoon garlic powder

¼ teaspoon onion powder

½ cup (45 g) sliced almonds, lightly toasted

Add the cashews to a pot and fill the pot with enough water to cover the nuts by 3 inches (13 cm). Bring to a boil. Reduce to a simmer and simmer for 1 hour. Drain all excess water and cool the cashews. (You can cool them under cool running water.)

Add the cashews, yogurt, nutritional yeast, chia seeds, miso, oil, lemon juice, salt, and pepper to a food processor or high-speed blender. Purée until very smooth. If you have a blender that has a strong enough motor, you can let it run on high speed for 2 to 3 minutes. If needed, stop to scrape down the sides occasionally. The final product should be the texture of thick, creamy peanut butter. Transfer to a mixing bowl and fold in all the remaining ingredients, except for sliced almonds.

Divide the mixture into 2 equal portions. Place each portion in the center of a square of plastic wrap and wrap into a log shape. Place in the freezer for at least 2 hours to harden. This step is necessary to make the log firm enough to roll in the almonds. After it is rolled in the almonds it will keep its shape and can be rewrapped and kept in the refrigerator, as it is supposed to be a soft spreadable cheese.

Place the almonds on a plate. Once hardened, carefully unwrap a log and roll in the toasted almonds until coated. Serve, or rewrap and place back into the refrigerator until ready to serve.

YIELD: 2 logs, approximately 1 pound (454 g)

Cashew Potato Queso

▶ **NUT**: CASHEW ▶ OIL-FREE POTENTIAL ▶ SOY-FREE POTENTIAL ▶ GLUTEN-FREE POTENTIAL

This makes a ton of queso. Perfect for putting in a slow cooker to keep warm at a get-together. It's also pretty awesome to stir in a can (or two) of your favorite vegan chili. You can also pack it up in jars and keep it refrigerated (or frozen) until you are ready to use it. Or cut the recipe in half and you will still have plenty of queso to last for several dip and chip sessions. If you want to save time, you can stir in some of your favorite salsa at the end instead of chopping up all of those fresh veggies.

1½ pounds (24 ounces, or 681 g) peeled red potatoes, cubed

2 cups (224 g) cashews, soaked overnight or boiled, rinsed and drained

1 cup (235 ml) vegetable broth (for dip, add more for sauce)

¼ cup (30 g) nutritional yeast

¼ cup (60 ml) vegetable oil (optional)

2 tablespoons (30 ml) fresh lime juice

½ teaspoon ground turmeric

½ teaspoon paprika

¼ to ½ teaspoon chipotle powder or cayenne, to taste

¾ teaspoon ground cumin

1 cup (252 g) finely diced tomatoes

½ cup (50 g) finely diced scallion

½ cup (80 g) finely diced red onion

1 whole fresh jalapeño, finely diced (seeded or not)

Salt and pepper

Add the potatoes to a large pot of water and bring to a boil. Boil until very tender. Drain. Add the boiled potatoes and the rest of the ingredients through the cumin, to a blender. Purée until silky smooth. Add additional vegetable broth to get to your desired consistency (less for dip or more for sauce). Stir in the remaining ingredients. Store in an airtight container up to 2 weeks in the refrigerator and indefinitely in the freezer.

To use, add the desired amount to a microwave-safe dish. Heat on high in 30-second intervals, stirring in between, until warmed through. Alternatively, place in a pot and heat over low heat, constantly stirring, until warmed through. You can also add it to a slow cooker, heat to desired temperature, then switch to low or keep warm.

YIELD: 5 cups (1175 ml)

3

CHEERS TO NUT-RITIOUS MORNINGS

A New Morning Meal in Your View

If there's anything nuts and seeds are already renowned for, it's for being frequent guests at the morning table. We've all enjoyed the simple PB&J, a handful of toasted nuts tossed haphazardly into a bowl of oatmeal, trail mix stirred into a cup of yogurt, or a freshly baked almond croissant. We're expanding on their amazing abilities here by creating new, delicious recipes that go far beyond the usual (albeit super tasty) basics. Whether you're vegan or not, a good nut-based breakfast guarantees a solid start to your day. (Even if it doesn't necessarily guarantee that the commute to work will be any easier.)

Plum or Apricot Almond Crisp

▶ **NUT**: ALMOND ▶ GLUTEN-FREE POTENTIAL ▶ OIL-FREE ▶ SOY-FREE POTENTIAL

This breakfast treat is fantastic served with a big glass of nut milk, or scooped on top of some plain or vanilla vegan yogurt. It's also great-tasting enough to be enjoyed as is without accompaniment, or to masquerade as a dessert item with a nice scoop of vegan vanilla ice cream for decoration.

22 ounces (620 g) fresh red plums, apricots, or pluots

⅓ cup (106 g) pure maple syrup

⅓ cup (85 g) roasted crunchy or creamy almond butter

⅓ cup (80 ml) unsweetened plain almond milk

1 teaspoon pure vanilla extract

1 teaspoon ground cardamom

Pinch fine sea salt

⅔ cup (53 g) old-fashioned rolled oats

⅓ cup (40 g) almond meal

Dry-roasted almonds, coarsely chopped (optional)

Cut your fruit into quarters and remove the pits. Cut each quarter in two equal slices, then chop each in half lengthwise.

Preheat the oven to 350°F (180°C, or gas mark 4). Place the chopped fruit evenly at the bottom of an 8 x 10-inch (20 x 25 cm) baking pan. (A 9-inch, or 23 cm, square pan will work, too.)

In a medium bowl, whisk to combine the maple syrup, almond butter, milk, vanilla, cardamom, and salt. Place the oats and almond meal on top, and stir to thoroughly combine. Place evenly on top of the apricots. Bake for 40 minutes, until the top is golden brown. Let stand at least 15 minutes before serving. Sprinkle with chopped almonds, if desired. Serve warm or at room temperature.

YIELD: 4 servings

Recipe Note

Word of caution to bona fide sweet-toothed foodies out there: If you don't like the slight tartness of cooked plums or apricots, consider combining them with 1 to 2 tablespoons (12 to 24 g) of your favorite vegan granulated sugar before placing them at the bottom of the dish.

Peanut Butter Farina

▶ **NUT**: PEANUT ▶ GLUTEN-FREE POTENTIAL ▶ OIL-FREE ▶ QUICK AND EASY
▶ SOY-FREE POTENTIAL

Celine used to love eating *riz au lait* (a custardy rice pudding) as a youngster, and she was thrilled to notice that the richness and mellowness of peanut butter yield a doppelgänger result here.

3 cups (705 ml) unsweetened plain cashew, almond, or other nut milk

⅔ cup (109 g) brown rice farina (or other farina, such as wheat)

⅓ cup (85 g) natural crunchy or creamy peanut butter

¼ cup (80 g) pure maple syrup or agave nectar, to taste

½ teaspoon ground cinnamon

Pinch salt

½ teaspoon pure vanilla extract

Pour the milk in a large pot, and bring to a gentle boil on medium-high heat. Lower the heat and slowly whisk in the farina, stirring constantly to avoid lumps. Stir the peanut butter, maple syrup, and cinnamon into the farina. If the peanut butter you use is unsalted, add a tiny pinch of salt now. Simmer uncovered and stir occasionally until thickened and tender, about 8 minutes. Remove from the heat, and stir the vanilla into the farina. Cover and let stand at least 10 minutes before serving. The farina can also be served at room temperature. Slowly reheat leftovers on the stove with a splash of milk, if needed.

YIELD: 4 to 6 servings

Recipe Notes

• Not a fan of peanut butter? You can replace it with any nut butter you like, but note that the flavor profile will, of course, change as well.

• If you're in a decadent mood, add some chopped vegan chocolate on top. A few slices of banana or berries would also be nice garnishes, but we personally love it as is.

Mango Strawberry Cashew Oats

▸ **NUT**: CASHEW ▸ GLUTEN-FREE POTENTIAL ▸ OIL-FREE ▸ SOY-FREE POTENTIAL

The modest amount of cashew butter used in this fruity, hot breakfast is actually enough to make for a creamy, rich, and filling bowl of oats. We love the colorful and tasty contrast of the dried and fresh fruit additions here!

¾ cup (120 g) dry steel-cut oats

1½ cups (355 ml) unsweetened plain cashew or other nut milk

1½ cups (355 ml) water

2 tablespoons (32 g) roasted cashew butter

⅓ cup (66 g) packed chopped soft dried mango

2 tablespoons (40 g) pure maple syrup or other liquid natural vegan sweetener

½ teaspoon ginger powder or 2 teaspoons (4 g) grated fresh ginger

Pinch salt

½ teaspoon pure vanilla extract

1 cup (166 g) sliced fresh strawberries

Fresh mango chunks, for garnish (optional)

Toasted coconut flakes, for garnish (optional)

Toasted cashews, for garnish (optional)

Place the oats, milk, water, cashew butter, dried mango, maple syrup, ginger, and salt in a medium pot. Bring to a low boil, then lower the heat to a simmer. Cover and simmer for 30 minutes, stirring frequently. Adjust the heat as needed to prevent scorching, and keep an extra close eye on the oats near the end of cooking as scorching risks do increase.

Stir the vanilla into the oatmeal once ready. Let stand 10 minutes on the counter, with the lid still on. Top with strawberries, fresh mango, coconut, and cashews, and serve.

YIELD: 3 to 4 servings

Multigrain Hot Cereal with Nuts and Cherries

▶ **NUTS**: ALMOND, WALNUT, AND PECAN ▶ QUICK AND EASY ▶ SOY-FREE POTENTIAL
▶ OIL-FREE POTENTIAL

Hearty, warm, and cozy, this cereal has a hint of tart from the cherries and just enough sweetness from the maple syrup. It is quick to put together—and it puts those instant packets to shame.

1 quart (4 cups, or 940 ml) water

¼ teaspoon salt

1 cup (78 g) quick-cooking rolled oats

⅓ cup (65 g) amaranth

⅓ cup (56 g) quinoa

⅓ cup (47 g) bulgur wheat

1 cup (128 g) dried cherries, chopped

⅓ cup (30 g) sliced or (36 g) slivered almonds

⅓ cup (40 g) chopped walnuts

⅓ cup (37 g) chopped pecans

⅓ cup (106 g) pure maple syrup, to taste

⅓ cup (80 ml) almond milk

1 tablespoon (15 ml) pure vanilla extract

Bring the water and salt to a boil. Stir in the oats, amaranth, quinoa, and bulgur wheat. Boil for 7 to 10 minutes, stirring often, until the tails on the quinoa spring and the grains are tender. Remove from the heat and stir in the remaining ingredients. Serve immediately.

YIELD: 6 servings

Recipe Note

You can refrigerate any leftovers and reheat with no problems. Just add a little extra almond milk when reheating.

Pão de Nozes (Nut Bread)

▶ **NUT AND SEED**: WALNUT OR PECAN AND CHIA ▶ SOY-FREE POTENTIAL

Perk up your morning ritual! An army of crunchy nuts make for a delightful, whole-grain bread that is tender and perfect to slice. Toasted (or not), with the addition of nut or seed butter (or not)—there's just no wrong way to enjoy it.

Nonstick cooking spray or oil spray

2 tablespoons (20 g) chia seeds

½ cup (120 ml) unfiltered, unsweetened apple cider (not hard cider) or apple juice

2 cups (240 g) whole wheat pastry flour

1 tablespoon (12 g) baking powder

1 teaspoon ground cinnamon

½ teaspoon fine sea salt

1 cup (109 g) coarsely chopped toasted pecans or (120 g) coarsely chopped toasted walnuts

¾ cup plus 2 tablespoons (210 ml) unsweetened plain almond or other nut milk

¾ cup plus 2 tablespoons (168 g) Sucanat

2 tablespoons (30 ml) roasted walnut or pecan oil (or any vegetable oil)

1½ teaspoons pure vanilla extract

Preheat the oven to 350°F (180°C, or gas mark 4). Coat an 8 x 4-inch (20 x 10 cm) loaf pan with cooking spray. Combine the chia seeds with the juice in a medium bowl with a whisk. Set aside for 5 minutes. In a large bowl, whisk to combine the flour, baking powder, cinnamon, and salt. Add the nuts on top. Add the milk, Sucanat, oil, and vanilla on top of the chia mixture. Whisk to combine.

Pour the wet ingredients into the dry, and stir to combine with a rubber spatula. Pour the batter into the prepared pan, and bake 55 minutes, or until a toothpick inserted in the center of the cake comes out dry. Loosely cover with a piece of foil if the loaf browns too quickly. Turn off the oven and leave the loaf in the oven for another 5 minutes.

Remove from the oven, and place on a wire rack. Wait 5 minutes before removing the loaf from the pan. Let cool completely before slicing. Store the leftovers in foil or in an airtight container at room temperature for up to 4 days. This loaf freezes exceptionally well for up to 3 months, tightly wrapped in foil.

YIELD: 1 loaf

Ginger or Lemon Tahini Scones

▶ **SEED**: SESAME ▶ SOY-FREE POTENTIAL

We've been fond of using tahini paste in baked goods for quite a few years now. There's just something about the buttery flavor it imparts that we can't get enough of. Its appearance in these unusual and elegant scones doesn't disappoint! Serve them with all-fruit blueberry (or other berry) preserves, or vegan lemon curd.

⅔ cup (160 ml) unsweetened plain vegan milk (any kind)

2 tablespoons (40 g) pure maple syrup or agave nectar

¼ cup (64 g) tahini paste

2 cups plus 1 tablespoon (250 g) whole spelt flour

1 teaspoon quick-rise yeast

1 tablespoon (8 g) roasted sesame seeds

½ teaspoon coarse kosher salt

¼ cup (40 g) diced crystallized ginger or preserved lemons (rinsed, patted dry, pulp sliced off, chopped rind)

¼ cup (30 g) chopped dates

½ teaspoon melted coconut oil

3 tablespoons (36 g) turbinado sugar (optional, for a crunchy exterior)

Combine the milk, maple syrup, and tahini in a small saucepan. Heat on medium heat until just lukewarm. In a large bowl, combine the flour, yeast, sesame seeds, and salt. Add the ginger or lemon, and dates on top. Pour the lukewarm mixture on top, and stir to combine. Use a stand mixer fitted with a dough hook, or knead by hand on a lightly floured surface, for a total of 8 minutes or until the dough is workable and cohesive. Lightly coat a large bowl with the coconut oil, and turn the dough around to coat. Cover tightly with a lid or plastic wrap, and let stand 80 minutes. Don't be concerned if the rise isn't impressive at this stage.

Place the sugar in a shallow plate. Pat down the dough into an 8-inch (20 cm) circle on a silicone baking mat. Cut it into 8 equal, triangular pieces, flattening each slightly. Dip each scone in the sugar, on every side. Place the scones back on the baking mat, and transfer to a baking sheet. Let stand uncovered for about 10 minutes, while preheating the oven to 400°F (200°C, or gas mark 6). Bake 16 to 18 minutes, or until golden brown. Transfer to a wire rack for 20 minutes, and serve. These are best fresh, but can be reheated in the oven.

YIELD: 8 scones

Recipe Note

The flavor of preserved lemons is reminiscent of candied lemon peel in this recipe. If it isn't something you like or if you have trouble finding them, choose ginger instead.

Hazelnut Chocolate Chip Muffins

▶ **NUT AND SEED**: HAZELNUT AND CHIA ▶ SOY-FREE POTENTIAL

There's nothing quite like a nice, sweet muffin for breakfast or as a snack. We're really thrilled by how pleasantly soft yet sturdy these puppies came out. If you want to make yours extra hazelnut-y, be sure to see the Recipe Note below.

¾ cup (180 ml) fresh orange juice

2 tablespoons (20 g) chia seeds

¾ cup (144 g) Sucanat

2 tablespoons (30 ml) neutral-flavored vegetable oil

1 teaspoon ground cinnamon

1 teaspoon pure vanilla extract

¼ teaspoon coarse kosher salt

1¼ cups (150 g) whole wheat pastry flour

¾ cup (90 g) hazelnut meal

1½ teaspoons baking powder

¼ cup (60 g) mini vegan semisweet chocolate chips or chopped chocolate

Preheat the oven to 350°F (180°C, or gas mark 4). Line a standard muffin tin with 10 paper liners. In a large bowl, whisk to combine the orange juice, chia seeds, Sucanat, oil, cinnamon, vanilla, and salt. Add the flour, hazelnut meal, baking powder, and chocolate chips on top. Stir to thoroughly combine.

Divide the batter among the liners, a generous three-quarters of the way up. Bake for 22 minutes, until the muffins are light golden brown around the edges, and firm on top. Transfer to a wire rack to cool. Store leftovers in an airtight container at room temperature for up to 1 day.

YIELD: 10 muffins

Recipe Note

We love to add a few shelled, raw, whole hazelnuts on top of the batter before baking: they get perfectly toasted and add an extra boost to the hazelnut flavor here. You could also coarsely chop ¼ cup to ⅓ cup (34 to 45 g) toasted hazelnuts and add them directly to the batter. Or if you are in a decadent mood, prepare some of Joni's Almond Cocoa Drizzle (page 170) with hazelnut butter and milk, without thinning it out even if it's thick, and drizzle or spread it on top of the cooled muffins.

CocoAlmond Waffles

▶ **NUT**: ALMOND ▶ SOY-FREE POTENTIAL ▶ GLUTEN-FREE POTENTIAL

These waffles are rich and decadent with chocolate, coconut, and almonds playing nicely together for a sophisticated, yet fun, twist on this classic breakfast treat.

2 cups (470 ml) almond milk

2 tablespoons (30 ml) fresh lemon juice

½ cup (60 g) shredded coconut

¾ cup (72 g) almond flour

¾ cup (74 g) coconut flour

¼ cup (30 g) oat flour

¼ cup (20 g) unsweetened cocoa powder

3 tablespoons (24 g) cornstarch

1 teaspoon baking powder

½ teaspoon baking soda

½ teaspoon salt

⅓ cup (73 g) brown sugar

⅓ cup (80 ml) melted coconut oil

1 teaspoon pure vanilla extract

1 teaspoon almond extract

1 teaspoon instant coffee crystals

½ cup sliced (45 g) or slivered almonds (54 g), toasted

½ cup (88 g) vegan chocolate chips or chunks

Pure maple syrup, to taste

Place the almond milk in a small dish. Stir in the lemon juice and set aside. It will curdle and become like buttermilk.

In a medium bowl, mix together the shredded coconut with the almond, coconut, and oat flours. Mix in the cocoa powder, baking soda, baking powder, and salt.

In a separate bowl, stir together the brown sugar, coconut oil, vanilla and almond extracts, coffee crystals, and buttermilk mixture. Fold wet into dry and combine until well mixed.

Pour ½ cup (100 g) batter onto a well-oiled waffle maker and follow the directions for your machine. You may need more or less depending on the size of your waffle maker. Top with a sprinkle of toasted almonds and chocolate chips and, of course, a healthy dose of real maple syrup.

YIELD: 6 standard-size waffles

Almond Sticky Buns with Orange Glaze

▶ **NUT**: ALMOND ▶ SOY-FREE POTENTIAL

Almonds and orange with a hint of cinnamon play well off each other in this grown-up version of the cinnamon roll.

FOR THE STICKY BUNS:

1 cup (235 ml) water, heated to lukewarm

2 tablespoons (24 g) turbinado sugar

1½ teaspoons (¼ ounce, or 7 g) active dry yeast

2 cups (240 g) whole wheat pastry flour

¼ teaspoon ground cinnamon

¼ teaspoon salt

¼ cup (64 g) almond butter

½ teaspoon pure almond extract

½ teaspoon pure vanilla extract

½ teaspoon mild vegetable oil

To make the sticky buns: Combine the water with the sugar. Stir in the yeast and let sit a few minutes until bubbles appear, to ensure the yeast is active. In a large bowl, combine the flour, cinnamon, and salt. Add the almond butter, almond extract, and vanilla to the yeast mixture. Stir the yeast mixture into dry, mixing until combined.

Lightly flour the counter, place the dough onto the counter, and start kneading. If the dough is too dry, add a smidge more water as needed. If it is too wet, add a smidge more flour as needed. Knead for 8 minutes, until the dough is smooth and pliable. Alternatively, use a stand mixer fitted with the dough hook. The kneading time will be the same, until the dough forms a ball.

Lightly coat a large bowl with ½ teaspoon of oil. Place the dough in bowl and gently roll and turn the dough to coat with oil. Cover tightly with plastic wrap, and let rise until doubled, 60 to 90 minutes. Gently deflate dough and place on a lightly floured surface. Knead for an additional 3 to 5 minutes.

Preheat the oven to 350°F (180°C, or gas mark 4). Line a baking sheet with parchment or a silicone baking mat. On a well-floured surface, roll the dough out into a 12 x 16-inch (30 x 40 cm) rectangle.

FOR THE FILLING:

¼ cup (56 g) coconut oil

2 tablespoons (32 g) almond butter

1 cup (220 g) firmly packed brown sugar

½ teaspoon ground cinnamon

½ cup (45 g) sliced almonds

FOR THE GLAZE:

1½ cups (180 g) powdered sugar, sifted

¼ cup (60 ml) fresh orange juice

Zest of one orange

¼ cup (23 g) sliced almonds

To make the filling: Mash together the coconut oil, almond butter, brown sugar, and cinnamon using your hands to make a well incorporated paste. Spread the filling in an even layer across the dough. Then sprinkled the sliced almonds evenly all over the filling. Starting at the short end of the rectangle, roll up the dough tightly. Using a sharp knife, cut the rolled-up dough into 12 equal sticky buns.

Place on the baking sheet, equally spaced from each other. Allow to sit for about 20 minutes before baking. Bake for 16 to 18 minutes, or until golden brown. While the sticky buns are baking, prepare the glaze.

To make the glaze: Whisk together the powdered sugar and orange juice. Set aside. Have the orange zest and sliced almonds ready. Once the sticky buns are done, allow to cool for a few minutes before brushing the entire top with glaze. Sprinkle the orange zest and sliced almonds all over the top. Serve warm.

YIELD: 1 dozen sticky buns

Cashew Pistachio Granola

▶ **NUTS AND SEEDS**: CASHEW, PISTACHIO, AND CHIA ▶ GLUTEN-FREE POTENTIAL
▶ SOY-FREE POTENTIAL

Awaken your still-sleepy taste buds with loads of crunch and flavor! This beautifully colored granola is great served with nut milk (unsweetened cashew milk is our favorite here) or on top of your favorite plain vegan yogurt. We've made the turmeric optional, but it's so good: It makes for a nice hue and also adds warm flavor.

2½ cups (240 g) old-fashioned rolled oats

2 tablespoons (20 g) chia seeds

1 teaspoon ginger powder

1 teaspoon ground cinnamon

1 teaspoon ground turmeric (optional)

½ teaspoon coarse kosher salt

¼ cup (64 g) roasted cashew butter (at room temperature for easy stirring)

¼ cup (80 g) brown rice syrup or agave nectar

¼ cup (48 g) coconut sugar or Sucanat

2 tablespoons (30 ml) roasted pistachio oil or melted coconut oil (see Recipe Notes)

1 teaspoon pure vanilla extract

½ cup (70 g) dry-roasted cashew pieces

⅓ cup (47 g) chopped soft dried mango

⅓ cup (53 g) chopped dried Turkish apricots

¼ cup (30 g) shelled dry-roasted pistachios

Preheat the oven to 300°F (150°C, or gas mark 2). Line a large, rimmed baking sheet lined with a silicone baking mat or parchment paper.

Combine the oats, chia seeds, ginger, cinnamon, turmeric, and salt in a large bowl. In a small bowl, stir to combine the cashew butter, syrup, sugar, oil, and vanilla. Pour the wet ingredients on top, stirring to thoroughly combine.

Place the granola in an even layer on the prepared sheet. Bake until it is golden brown and smells toasty, about 30 minutes, carefully flipping with a large spatula approximately every 10 minutes. Remove from the oven and let cool on the sheet. The granola will crisp up as it cools. Stir the cashews, mango, apricots, and pistachios into the cooled granola. Store in an airtight container at room temperature for up to 2 weeks.

YIELD: 6 cups (660 g)

Recipe Notes

• If using melted coconut oil instead of pistachio oil, be sure that all the ingredients are at room temperature before stirring or the coconut oil will harden, making mixing a difficult task. If this sounds like a hassle, you can use grapeseed or olive oil.

• Adding a few tablespoons to taste (10 g per tablespoon) of diced candied ginger is a great option for an extra kick of flavor.

Peanut Butter French Toast with Maple Pecan Dipping Sauce

▶ **NUTS**: PEANUT AND PECAN   ▶ SOY-FREE POTENTIAL   ▶ QUICK AND EASY

This is a great breakfast treat when you have a big family, or the kids are having a sleepover, or you want to make a fun, casual breakfast. If you want to make a smaller batch, feel free. The dipping sauce is made with equal parts maple syrup and peanut butter, so adjust accordingly.

FOR THE PEANUT BUTTER FRENCH TOAST:

Day-old French baguettes (you can use any type of bread, but we like French bread for French toast!)

1½ cups (180 g) whole wheat pastry flour, or all-purpose flour (185 g), spooned and leveled

¼ cup (24 g) powdered peanut butter

½ teaspoon ground cinnamon

¼ teaspoon salt

1½ cups (355 ml) nut milk

Oil for frying

Powdered sugar, for garnish (optional)

FOR THE MAPLE PECAN DIPPING SAUCE:

½ cup (120 ml) pure maple syrup

½ cup (128 g) peanut butter

⅓ cup (37 g) chopped pecans, roasted or toasted

To make the French toast: First cut the baguette on the bias into slices 1 inch (2.5 cm) thick. Mix together the flour, powdered peanut butter, cinnamon, and salt in a medium mixing bowl. Mix in the nut milk and stir until well combined. The consistency should be that of a pancake batter.

Add enough oil to a frying pan to equal ½ inch (1.3 cm) deep and preheat the oil to 350°F (180°C). Line a platter or plate with paper towels to absorb excess oil.

Dip a slice of baguette into the batter and remove excess batter. Carefully add the battered bread to the oil and fry until golden; flip and repeat with the other side. Carefully remove from the pan and transfer to the lined platter. Repeat with the remaining slices until all the batter is used. Garnish with a sprinkle of powdered sugar, if desired.

To make the dipping sauce: Stir together the maple syrup and peanut butter until well combined. Fold in the pecans. If you are using raw pecans, chop them, then lightly toast them in a dry pan. This process doesn't take long, so be careful not to burn your nuts! Serve on a plate with a small dish for dipping. Alternatively, you can serve traditionally with the dipping sauce drizzled all over the top.

YIELD: Servings will vary, depending on the size of your baguettes and how small you cut them.

PB&J Breakfast Samosas

▶ **NUT**: PEANUT ▶ SOY-FREE POTENTIAL ▶ OIL-FREE POTENTIAL (BAKED VERSION ONLY)

These handheld pockets of goodness are a great replacement for those toaster pastries that start with a Pop and end with a Tart. They can be made two ways: bake 'em or fry 'em. The addition of beans gives these an extra protein and fiber punch to get you through your busy day. If you're not feeling bean-y, leave it out and just fill your samosas with nut butter and jam.

½ cup (62 g) all-purpose flour

½ cup (120 ml) water

4 (6-inch, or 15 cm) vegan flour tortillas

1 can (15 ounces, or 425 g) white beans, drained and rinsed (optional)

½ cup (128 g) peanut butter or any nut butter of choice, divided

½ cup (120 ml) nut milk of choice, divided

½ cup (160 g) your favorite jam or jelly

2 tablespoons (24 g) granulated raw sugar

½ teaspoon ground cinnamon

Oil for frying (optional)

Mix together the flour and water into a paste in a small bowl and set aside. Cut your tortillas in half. Add the beans (if using), peanut butter, and ¼ cup (60 ml) of the milk to a blender. Purée until smooth. Have jam or jelly at the ready. Mix together sugar and cinnamon in a small bowl, and set aside.

Lay one tortilla half on a flat work surface with the straight edge on top. Fold the left corner down to the center of the rounded edge. Repeat with the right corner to form a triangle. Glue the two straight edges together using a line of flour paste spread onto the tortilla with your finger. Fill the pocket with 2 tablespoons (35 g) of the peanut butter–bean mixture and 1 tablespoon (20 g) of the jam. Seal the pouch closed with another line of flour paste.

To Bake: Preheat the oven to 350°F (180°C, or gas mark 4). Line a baking sheet with parchment or a reusable baking mat. Arrange the samosas on the tray and brush with the remaining milk. Sprinkle liberally with the cinnamon and sugar mix. Bake for 8 to 10 minutes, or until golden around the edges and the sugar has melted onto the samosas.

To Fry: Preheat the oil to 350°F (180°C). Fill a small pot with 2 inches (5 cm) of oil or use your deep fat fryer. Line a plate with paper towels to absorb excess oil after frying. Carefully add one samosa to the oil and fry for 1 minute, or until golden and crispy. Carefully flip and repeat on the other side. Transfer to the paper towel–lined tray. Sprinkle with the cinnamon and sugar mix.

Allow to cool before serving.

YIELD: 8 samosas

Banana-Nut-Bread Pancakes

▶ **NUT AND SEED**: WALNUT AND FLAX ▶ SOY-FREE POTENTIAL

Everything you love about banana nut bread, but in a pancake.

FOR THE PANCAKES:

1 cup (235 ml) nut milk

1 tablespoon (15 ml) fresh lemon juice

½ cup (60 g) whole wheat pastry flour

¾ cup (93 g) all-purpose flour

1 tablespoon (7 g) ground flaxseed

1 teaspoon baking powder

¼ teaspoon baking soda

¼ teaspoon salt

⅛ teaspoon ground cinnamon

3 tablespoons (41 g) brown sugar

2 tablespoons (30 ml) melted coconut oil

1 teaspoon pure vanilla extract

1 ripe banana, mashed

½ cup (60 g) chopped walnuts

FOR THE TOPPING:

1 banana, sliced

½ cup (60 g) chopped walnuts

Warmed pure maple syrup, to taste

In a small bowl, add the nut milk and lemon juice. Set aside. It will curdle and become like buttermilk. In a separate bowl, mix together the whole wheat pastry flour, all-purpose flour, ground flaxseed, baking powder, baking soda, salt, and cinnamon.

Add the brown sugar, melted coconut oil, vanilla, and mashed banana to the buttermilk mixture. Stir to combine. Add the wet to dry and mix until well incorporated. Fold in the chopped walnuts. Allow to rest 15 minutes before cooking.

Heat a nonstick or cast-iron skillet over medium heat. Using a ⅓-cup measure (3.25 ounces, or 92 g), pour the batter onto the griddle and cook as you would any pancake, or until bubbles begin to pop and edges begin to lift, then flip. Repeat with the remaining batter. To serve, top with the sliced banana, chopped walnuts, and warmed maple syrup.

YIELD: 6 to 8 pancakes

Strawberry Almond Horchata

▶ **NUT**: ALMOND ▶ GLUTEN-FREE POTENTIAL ▶ OIL-FREE ▶ SOY-FREE POTENTIAL

Horchata is a creamy, rice-based Mexican drink, with various flavors added in. Here, we've added roasted almonds for a richer taste, and a touch of coconut cream for extra creaminess. The fruity, refreshing outcome is a welcome addition to the morning table!

½ cup (90 g) dry brown jasmine rice, rinsed and drained

½ cup (60 g) dry-roasted or raw almonds (skinned or not), to taste

4 cups (940 ml) filtered water, divided

¼ cup (60 g) chilled coconut cream

¾ cup (140 g) frozen strawberries

2 tablespoons (40 g) agave nectar or pure maple syrup, to taste

½ teaspoon pure vanilla extract

½ teaspoon pure rosewater, to taste (optional)

Pinch fine sea salt

Place the rice and almonds in a large glass measuring cup or other glass container, and cover with 2 cups (470 ml) filtered water, or enough to cover by about 2 inches (5 cm). Cover with a lid or plastic wrap, and let stand at room temperature for at least 8 hours, up to 22 hours.

Drain (discard the soaking water) and rinse well. Place in a blender or use an immersion blender, and cover with the remaining 2 cups (470 ml) water. Blend until the rice and almonds are completely broken down.

Place a fine-mesh sieve on top of a large glass measuring cup or bowl. Use a nut milk bag to strain the rice and almond milk, making sure to squeeze the bag to get all the liquid out. Do not discard the pulp! (See Recipe Note.)

Add the coconut cream, strawberries, agave, vanilla, rosewater (if using), and salt to the blender, along with the rice and almond milk mixture. Blend until thoroughly combined and smooth. Have a taste and add extra sweetener to taste if needed. Serve immediately: the frozen berries will take care of chilling the drink.

YIELD: Three 1-cup (235 ml) servings

Recipe Note

Make porridge out of the leftover pulp! Combine pulp in a saucepan with a pinch of salt and twice the amount of liquid (half water, half vegan milk) as pulp. Heat on medium-high, lower the heat, and simmer covered until thickened and tender, about 15 minutes (cooking time will vary), stirring occasionally. Add fresh or dried fruit, pure vanilla extract, cinnamon, and sweetener to taste.

Creamy Cashew Miso Oats

▶ **NUT AND SEED**: CASHEW AND SESAME ▶ GLUTEN-FREE POTENTIAL ▶ OIL-FREE

This mellow, buttery, risotto-like concoction was originally created to be a nutritious, savory breakfast item, but it's also fantastic as a light supper. Pick the garnishes you crave the most, and make this recipe your own! Props to Liz Wyman for coming up with the idea of serving these versatile oats with mushrooms for a savory boost.

1 cup (184 g) dry oat groats

1¾ cups plus 2 tablespoons (445 ml) water or mushroom broth, divided

¼ cup (64 g) roasted unsalted cashew butter (or any other nut or seed butter, preferably unsalted)

2 tablespoons (36 g) shiro (white) miso

1½ teaspoons fresh lemon juice

1 to 2 cloves garlic, grated or pressed, to taste

Garnishes: thinly sliced scallion (green parts only); sliced mushrooms of choice sautéed in tamari; thinly sliced pickled cucumber and carrot; sesame seeds; lemon wedges; brown rice vinegar; tamari

Place the oats in a large, glass measuring cup. Cover with an extra 2 inches (5 cm) filtered water, tightly cover with plastic wrap, and soak overnight (about 8 hours) at room temperature. Drain (discard the soaking water) and rinse thoroughly.

Place the oats in a large skillet, and cover with 1½ cups (355 ml) water. Cover and bring to a boil. Cook uncovered on medium heat for 10 minutes, stirring occasionally. Cover with a lid and simmer another 10 to 15 minutes, until the liquid is absorbed and the oats are al dente. If the oats are still too hard, you can add water as needed here. Stir occasionally.

Whisk together the remaining ¼ cup plus 2 tablespoons (90 ml) water, cashew butter, miso, lemon juice, and garlic.

Stir the miso mixture into the oats. Simmer partially covered until tender, thickened, and not soupy, about 10 minutes. Stir occasionally so as not to scorch. If the oats are not tender to taste, you can still add a little extra water here, but be sure not to boil in order to retain miso's healthy properties.

Turn off the stove and let stand covered for another 10 minutes. Serve each portion with garnishes of choice.

YIELD: 3 servings

Protein-Packed Breakfast Scramble

▶ **NUTS AND SEEDS**: PEPITA, CASHEW, ALMOND, HEMP HEART, AND FLAX
▶ QUICK AND EASY ▶ OIL-FREE POTENTIAL ▶ GLUTEN-FREE POTENTIAL

A nutty take on your 'fu scram. Eat it as is, wrap it up in a tortilla for an on-the-go breakfast wrap, or top a bowl of brown rice with it for a really, really hearty meal.

1 can (15 ounces, or 425 g) chickpeas, with the liquid

1 block (8 ounces, or 227 g) extra or super firm tofu (we prefer smoked tofu in this recipe), drained and pressed

⅓ cup (21 g) pepitas

½ cup (56 g) cashews

¼ cup (27 g) slivered almonds

¼ cup (40 g) hemp hearts (hemp seeds with shells removed)

1 tablespoon (7 g) whole flaxseed

1 tablespoon (10 g) minced garlic

½ teaspoon Dijon mustard

½ teaspoon ground turmeric

¼ teaspoon ground cumin

¼ teaspoon paprika

4 ounces (112 g) baby spinach

¼ teaspoon black salt (kala namak)

Salt and pepper

Heat a large, nonstick frying pan or well-seasoned cast-iron skillet over medium heat. Add in the chickpeas and liquid and begin to cook. While the beans are cooking, cube the tofu into small bite-size pieces. (Some prefer them cubed, and some of y'all prefer to crumble your 'fu, so do as you please.)

Add the tofu to the pan. Stir in the seeds, nuts, garlic, mustard, and spices, and mix to combine. Continue to cook and toss until all the ingredients are coated and heated through and most of the liquid has been absorbed or evaporated. Turn off the heat; stir in the spinach and black salt. Add salt and pepper to taste.

YIELD: 4 meal-size servings or 8 side-dish servings

Cashew Butter and Sesame Tomato Jam on Toast

▶ **NUT AND SEED**: CASHEW AND SESAME ▶ SOY-FREE POTENTIAL

Artisan toast is all the rage these days and this one fits the bill nicely. This simple breakfast can be made quickly if you make the Tomato Jam ahead of time. If you are gluten-sensitive, this recipe can be easily made gluten free by choosing gluten-free bread for the toast.

FOR THE SESAME TOMATO JAM:

1 can (15 ounces, or 425 g) diced tomatoes, with their juices

½ cup (80 g) diced red onion

1 tablespoon (22 g) molasses

2 teaspoons (10 ml) sesame oil

2 teaspoons (6 g) minced garlic

1 teaspoon sambal oelek

1 teaspoon sesame seeds (white or black, or both!)

¼ teaspoon salt, to taste

¼ teaspoon black pepper, to taste

FOR EACH SLICE OF TOAST:

1 slice of bread

1 tablespoon (16 g) cashew butter

¼ of an avocado, sliced (optional)

2 tablespoons (40 g) Sesame Tomato Jam

Salt and pepper

Chopped cilantro, for garnish (optional)

Chopped scallion, for garnish (optional)

To make the Sesame Tomato Jam: Add all the ingredients to a sauce pot and stir to combine. Bring to a simmer over medium-high heat and simmer 20 to 25 minutes, or until most of the liquid has been absorbed and you are left with a thick jam-like spread. Stir continuously. Cool completely and store in an airtight container in the refrigerator until ready to serve.

To make the toast: Toast the bread, spread each slice of bread with cashew butter. Add slices of avocado, if desired. Then add the Sesame Tomato Jam. Sprinkle on salt and pepper to taste. Garnish with cilantro and scallion, if desired, and serve.

YIELD: 1½ cups (480 g) Sesame Tomato Jam

Cashew and Seeds Sandwich Bread

▶ **NUT AND SEEDS**: CASHEW, PEPITA, CHIA, AND FLAX ▶ SOY-FREE POTENTIAL

This bread is packed with nuts and seeds! If you want to go overboard (in the best possible way), you know you'll want to toast a slice or two and spread even more nut or seed butter on top.

1½ cups (180 g) whole spelt flour, plus extra for kneading and dusting

1½ cups (180 g) whole wheat bread flour or regular bread flour (see Recipe Note)

1½ teaspoons quick-rise yeast

1 generous teaspoon fine sea salt

¼ cup (30 g) roasted pepitas

2 tablespoons (20 g) chia seeds

2 tablespoons (15 g) golden roasted flaxseeds

1 cup (235 ml) lukewarm unsweetened plain cashew milk

¼ cup (64 g) roasted cashew butter

1 tablespoon (20 g) brown rice syrup, regular molasses, or pure maple syrup

Nonstick cooking spray or oil spray

Recipe Note

If bread flour isn't available, use the same amount of either all-purpose flour, or regular or white whole wheat flour instead.

In a large bowl, combine the flours, yeast, salt, pepitas, chia seeds, and flaxseeds. In a separate bowl, whisk to combine the milk, cashew butter, and syrup. Pour the wet ingredients into the flour bowl, and stir to combine with a wooden spoon or rubber spatula. Transfer the mixture to a lightly floured surface once it starts forming into a dough, and knead until a supple, cohesive dough forms, about 8 to 10 minutes. Alternatively, this can be done with a stand mixer, using a dough hook. Place the dough back into the bowl, cover tightly, and let stand until doubled, about 75 minutes.

Lightly coat an 8 x 4-inch (20 x 10 cm) loaf pan with cooking spray. Gently punch down the dough, flatten it with your hands or a rolling pin into a 9-inch (23 cm) square, and divide it into 3 equal parts. Roll up each part tightly and gather to form a single loaf, with 3 humps. Gently press down the loaf to fit the pan. Cover with plastic wrap, and let rise until doubled and slightly over the edges of the pan, about 40 minutes.

Preheat the oven to 375°F (190°C, or gas mark 5). Remove the plastic wrap, and place the bread into the oven (not too close to the burners as the dough will continue rising). Bake until golden brown, about 30 minutes. Remove from the pan, place on a cooling rack, and let cool completely before slicing.

YIELD: 1 loaf

4

SIMPLE NUTS MAKE MEAN MAINS

Seamlessly Going from Beloved Snack to Headliner of the Meal

Nuts and seeds are often used as an afterthought in many recipes, as a mere garnish, rather than as the inspiration for the meal. We've flipped this concept upside down by building fancy and colorful plant-based main dishes *around* the ultimate attraction of the show. Ladies and gentlemen, a round of applause for mighty nuts and seeds!

Cashew Cauliflower Curry with Quinoa

▶ **NUT**: CASHEW ▶ GLUTEN-FREE POTENTIAL ▶ SOY-FREE POTENTIAL

Still looking for more fast and tasty options for healthy meals in no time? Behold, this colorful curry that makes good use of that leftover cooked quinoa (or brown rice) hiding in the back of the fridge.

Black mustard seeds are quite fragrant, but can be hard to find. If you have brown mustard seeds, they will do the trick in a pinch even though they are not quite as pungent. Or you can leave them out entirely.

½ cup (70 g) raw whole cashews

1 tablespoon (15 ml) grapeseed, melted coconut, or olive oil

½ teaspoon black mustard seeds (see headnote)

3 cups (300 g) small cauliflower florets

1 bell pepper (any color), trimmed and cored, chopped

½ or 1 whole small habañero or other medium to hot pepper, seeded and minced, to taste (wear gloves)

2 small shallots, trimmed, peeled, and chopped

3 cloves garlic, minced

1 teaspoon mild to medium curry powder

1 teaspoon garam masala

½ teaspoon ginger powder or 1½ teaspoons grated fresh ginger

½ teaspoon ground cumin

½ teaspoon ground coriander

½ teaspoon fine sea salt, to taste

½ teaspoon ground turmeric

Juice of a quarter lime

½ cup (120 ml) unsweetened plain cashew milk (or other nut milk)

1¾ cups (324 g) cooked quinoa

Chopped fresh cilantro or parsley, to taste

Preheat the oven to 300°F (150°C, or gas mark 2). Place the cashews on a baking sheet. Bake until golden brown and fragrant, checking and stirring occasionally to prevent burning, about 10 to 15 minutes total. Set aside to cool.

Heat the oil in a large skillet over medium-high heat. Add the mustard seeds and cover with a lid. Be careful not to burn and carefully shake the pan occasionally, adjusting the heat if needed. After about 30 seconds, the sputtering will slow. Remove the lid. Add the cauliflower, and cook 6 minutes, until lightly browned. Add the peppers, shallots, and garlic, and cook uncovered for another 2 minutes. Add the curry powder, garam masala, ginger, cumin, coriander, salt, turmeric, and lime juice. Cook for another minute. Add the milk. Stir to combine, and cover with a lid. Cook for another 4 to 6 minutes, or until the cauliflower is tender. Remove the lid occasionally to stir. If the vegetables stick to the pan or if the curry isn't very saucy, add extra milk or vegetable broth as needed.

Serve on the quinoa, and sprinkle the cashews and herbs on top.

YIELD: 2 to 3 servings

Pistachio Orange Beet Pilaf

▶ **NUT**: PISTACHIO ▶ SOY-FREE POTENTIAL

Celine lives in a California town where sweltering summers are known to last for about six months. No wonder refreshing salads such as this one are an everyday occurrence in her household. The addition of a generous amount of pistachio nuts makes the salad a bit more substantial without weighing you down.

For the dressing, we usually go with 2 tablespoons (30 ml) orange juice, 1 tablespoon (15 ml) roasted pistachio oil, and 1 tablespoon (15 ml) white balsamic vinegar for the whole salad, with a pinch of salt. It all depends on how saucy you like it!

4 medium beets, trimmed and peeled, cut into bite-size cubes

1 to 2 teaspoons (5 to 10 g) harissa paste or (2 to 4 g) dry blend

⅜ teaspoon ground ginger or 1½ teaspoons grated peeled fresh ginger

¼ cup (60 ml) fresh orange juice, divided

1 scant teaspoon coarse kosher salt

2 shallots, peeled and quartered

1 cup (186 g) dry whole wheat couscous or (160 g) quick-cooking bulgur (not the soaking-only kind), cooked according to package directions

Roasted pistachio oil or extra-virgin olive oil

1 organic orange (for its zest)

White balsamic vinegar, as needed

½ cup (60 g) shelled pistachios, lightly roasted and coarsely chopped

¼ cup (about 15 g) fresh herbs (such as parsley, mint, or a combo)

Preheat the oven to 400°F (200°C, or gas mark 6). Place the beets, harissa, ginger, 2 tablespoons (30 ml) orange juice, salt, and shallots in a 9-inch (23 cm) square baking pan. Roast for a total of about 30 to 40 minutes, or until tender, stirring every 10 minutes. Set aside to cool to room temperature. Once cooled, chop the shallots.

To serve, divide the couscous or bulgur among 4 plates. Top with a quarter of the beets and shallot. Drizzle each serving with pistachio oil, 1½ teaspoons (of the remaining 2 tablespoons, or 30 ml) orange juice, a few grates of orange zest, and a drizzle of vinegar. Top with pistachios and herbs to taste. Serve immediately.

YIELD: 4 side-dish servings

Tahini Chickpea–Topped Rice and Carrot Bake

▶ **SEED**: SESAME (TAHINI) ▶ GLUTEN-FREE POTENTIAL

Big thumbs-up to the slightly cheesy, totally creamy, chickpea- and tahini-based topping on this healthy bake. We often serve it with a big salad tossed with a light vinaigrette for extra vegetable goodness. If you're out of pomegranate molasses, replace it with 1 tablespoon (15 ml) lemon juice and 1½ teaspoons agave nectar.

8 large carrots, trimmed and peeled, sliced into thin coins

½ large red onion, quartered

4 cloves garlic, peeled and left whole

1½ teaspoons ras el hanout

1 tablespoon (20 g) pomegranate molasses (page 17)

1 tablespoon (15 ml) olive oil

½ teaspoon harissa paste or dry blend

1 cup (188 g) dry brown rice of choice or 1 cup (170 g) dry quinoa, cooked

1 tablespoon (18 g) shiro (white) miso

2 tablespoons (30 ml) fresh lemon juice

¼ cup (64 g) tahini paste

2 tablespoons (15 g) nutritional yeast

1½ cups (256 g) cooked chickpeas

1 cup (235 ml) vegetable broth

Ground pepper

Roasted sesame seeds, for topping

Preheat the oven to 400°F (200°C, or gas mark 6). Place the carrots in a 9 x 13-inch (23 x 33 cm) baking pan, with the onion, garlic, ras el hanout, pomegranate molasses, oil, and harissa. Fold to combine. Roast in 10-minute increments, stirring after each increment, until the carrots are tender. Timing will vary with the freshness and variety of the carrots, but about 30 to 40 minutes.

In the meantime, evenly place the cooked rice at the bottom of a 9 x 13-inch (23 x 33 cm) baking pan. You can also use 4 smaller 6.5 x 5-inch (17 x 13 cm) baking dishes to make fancy individual bakes. If using the latter, stir the rice and carrots in a large bowl, then transfer to the dishes.

Place the miso, lemon juice, tahini, nutritional yeast, chickpeas, broth, and pepper in a blender. Blend until completely smooth. Set aside.

Once the carrots are ready and slightly cooled, you can chop the onion and mince the garlic; lower the oven heat to 375°F (190°C, or gas mark 5). Gently stir the carrots into the rice in the pan, using a rubber spatula. Evenly place the chickpea mixture on top of the carrots, and sprinkle with sesame seeds to taste. Bake for 25 minutes, or until the topping is set and slightly browned.

YIELD: 4 to 6 servings

Cajun Roasted Chestnuts and Potatoes

▶ **NUT**: CHESTNUT ▶ GLUTEN-FREE POTENTIAL ▶ SOY-FREE POTENTIAL

Fresh chestnuts can be hard to find when not in season: we have nothing against vacuum-packed, already-roasted chestnuts. If eaten as is, they aren't quite as scrumptious as fresh, but they still perform well when perfectly seasoned as in this recipe. Not having to do the peeling yourself is an added bonus. We use a salt-free Cajun seasoning blend, so be sure to adjust the quantity of salt if your seasoning isn't salt-free.

Nonstick cooking spray or oil spray

1 tablespoon (9 g) Cajun seasoning

1 tablespoon (15 ml) grapeseed, olive, or peanut oil

Juice 1 large lemon

1 teaspoon to 1 tablespoon (5 to 15 ml) hot sauce (Tabasco), to taste

1 pound (454 g) fingerling potatoes, halved or quartered depending on size

1 red bell pepper, trimmed, cored, quartered, each quarter cut into approximately 1-inch (2.5 cm) pieces

2 shallots (2 ounces, or 56 g once trimmed), quartered or 1 cup (90 g) sliced leek (thoroughly cleaned)

6 cloves garlic, left whole

1 scant cup (150 g) peeled roasted or steamed chestnuts

1 teaspoon coarse kosher salt (halve if not using a salt-free Cajun seasoning blend, or adjust to taste)

4 generous sprigs (4 g) fresh thyme

Preheat the oven to 400°F (200°C, or gas mark 6). Lightly coat a 9 x 13-inch (23 x 33 cm) baking pan with cooking spray.

In a large bowl, stir to combine the Cajun seasoning, oil, juice, and hot sauce. Add the potatoes, bell pepper, shallots, garlic, chestnuts, and salt. Stir, and add the thyme sprigs. Transfer to the prepared pan, and cover tightly with foil.

Roast for 15 minutes, then remove the foil to stir. Roast uncovered for another 10 minutes, then stir. Lower the heat to 350°F (180°C, or gas mark 4). Roast for another 10 minutes, or until the potatoes are tender. Turn off the oven, and leave the pan in there for another 5 minutes. Discard the thyme sprigs (the leaves should have fallen off). Mince the garlic and chop the shallots, and serve.

YIELD: 4 servings

Loaded Potatoes with Pepita Guacamole

▶ **NUT AND SEED**: ALMOND AND PEPITA ▶ GLUTEN-FREE POTENTIAL
▶ SOY-FREE POTENTIAL

These twice-baked potatoes with a creamy almond filling are piled high with vegetables, and they are almost too much fun to build and eat! When roasting the potatoes in a big oven instead of a countertop oven, we like to pair them with other foods that need roasting, such as garlic, bell peppers, or other vegetables. It makes the oven use more worthwhile as long as it doesn't get overly crowded in there.

2 large white or Russet potatoes (not peeled), halved lengthwise

Salt

Nonstick cooking spray or oil spray

⅓ cup plus 2 tablespoons (110 g) Almond Sour Cream (page 27)

2 tablespoons (10 g) minced scallion

1 large clove garlic, grated or pressed

½ jalapeño pepper (seeded or not), minced, to taste

1⅓ cups (93 g) finely shredded or chopped green cabbage

8 thin slices of tomato or 1 cup (180 g) fresh diced tomato (not canned)

1 recipe Pistachio Guacamole (page 32), made with pepitas and kept extra chunky

Lime wedges, for garnish

Pepitas, for garnish

Preheat the oven to 400°F (200°C, or gas mark 6). Lightly coat the flat half of each potato with cooking spray or oil and sprinkle a tiny pinch of salt on each. Place flat-side down on a small baking sheet and bake 45 minutes, then flip. Bake for another 15 minutes, or until tender. Lower the heat to 375°F (190°C, or gas mark 5).

Remove the potatoes from the oven. Let cool slightly until you can handle them to scoop out the flesh. Place the flesh in a bowl and coarsely mash. Stir with the sour cream, scallion, garlic, jalapeño pepper, and a generous pinch of salt. Divide the resulting preparation between each scooped-out potato, patting down to even out the tops. Place back on the baking sheet and bake until slightly golden, about 15 minutes. Prepare the guacamole while the potatoes are baking.

Add a generous handful (about ⅓ cup, or 23 g) cabbage on each potato half. Top with 2 tomato slices or ¼ cup (45 g) diced tomato, and one-quarter of the guacamole. Garnish with lime wedges. Top with a small handful of pepitas. Serve immediately.

YIELD: 4 filled potato halves

Zhoug Cashew Thin Omelets

▶ **NUT**: CASHEW OR ALMOND OR PISTACHIO ▶ GLUTEN-FREE POTENTIAL

Surprisingly filling and completely awesome, these omelets can be made with pretty much any nut, nut meal, and nut milk you want. We've tried them with cashews, almonds, and even pistachios, and loved every bite of each.

½ or 1 jalapeño pepper, trimmed and seeded, to taste

¼ cup (6 g) fresh cilantro leaves

¼ cup (15 g) fresh parsley leaves

3 scallions (about ½ cup, or 40 g)

2 cloves garlic, grated or pressed

1 tablespoon (15 ml) brown rice vinegar

1 tablespoon (15 ml) fresh lime juice

1 tablespoon (18 g) light miso

½ teaspoon ground cumin

¼ teaspoon ground black pepper, to taste

⅛ teaspoon ground cardamom

1 cup (235 ml) unsweetened plain cashew or almond milk

1 tablespoon (15 ml) grapeseed oil

¾ cup (90 g) garbanzo fava bean flour, sifted

¼ cup (30 g) cashew or almond or pistachio meal

2 tablespoons (15 g) nutritional yeast

¼ teaspoon baking powder

Scant ½ teaspoon coarse kosher salt

Nonstick cooking spray or oil spray

Place the pepper through the cardamom in a food processor. Pulse to combine, but leave slightly chunky. Transfer to a large bowl along with the milk and oil. Slowly whisk the flour, cashew meal, nutritional yeast, baking powder, and salt into the wet ingredients: there should be no flour lumps left. Let stand 15 minutes.

Heat a large, nonstick pan on medium-high heat. Lower the heat to medium. Lightly coat the pan with cooking spray or oil spray once hot, away from the heat. Add a scant ½ cup (110 ml) of batter to the skillet. The batter should spread itself to a thin, approximately 6.5-inch (16.5 cm) wide circle. Let cook for about 4 minutes, until the center looks not too dry but not too moist either. Carefully lift the edges of the omelet to make sure it is golden brown, which means it can be flipped. Carefully flip with a large spatula, and let cook for another 4 minutes, or until golden brown. Lightly coat the pan again each time before cooking the remaining 4 omelets. (We got 5 in all while some testers got 4, so the yield may vary.) Serve immediately.

YIELD: 2 to 4 servings

Ginger Soy Wasabi Toasted Almonds

▶ **NUT**: ALMOND ▶ QUICK AND EASY

These almonds taste great as a snack, but we need to smash the myth that nuts are only good for snacking! So try these awesome buggers on top of salads, in your tacos, to top your bowls, on the Thai Peanut Pizza (page 110), in wraps and sandwiches, even in your sushi rolls!

1 teaspoon wasabi powder

2 teaspoons (10 ml) water

1 tablespoon (14 g) coconut oil
(refined or unrefined is fine)

1 tablespoon (15 ml) soy sauce
(use gluten-free for a gluten-free dish)

2 teaspoons (6 g) sesame seeds,
black or white (or both!)

1 teaspoon garlic powder

½ teaspoon ginger powder

1 cup (108 g) slivered almonds

In a small bowl, mix together the wasabi powder and water. Let sit for 15 minutes to allow flavor to develop.

Add the coconut oil, soy sauce, sesame seeds, garlic powder, and ginger to the wasabi mixture and stir to mix.

Heat a frying pan over medium heat. Add the slivered almonds and lightly toast, 1 to 2 minutes. Add in the wet mixture and toss with the almonds. Reduce the heat to medium-low heat and continue to sauté until the majority of the liquid has been absorbed and the nuts are almost dry and sticky. Turn the nuts constantly to prevent burning.

Allow to cool completely before storing in an airtight container.

YIELD: 4 servings

Moroccan Pilaf with Pomegranate Walnuts

▶ **NUT**: WALNUT ▶ SOY-FREE POTENTIAL

We're always keen on recipes that are packed with various textures, a worthwhile amount of fiber-ful vegetables, and loads of flavors: this one definitely fits the bill. Just try not to eat all the walnuts while preparing the rest of the recipe—or make twice the amount needed if you're just as hopeless as we are.

FOR THE WALNUTS:

½ cup (60 g) walnut halves, broken in two

1 tablespoon (15 ml) pomegranate molasses (page 17), plus extra to serve

Generous pinch ground cumin or coriander

Pinch coarse kosher salt

FOR THE PILAF:

12 ounces (340 g) fresh broccoli florets

Generous pinch fine sea salt

2 cloves garlic (left whole)

1 tablespoon (15 ml) olive oil

½ habañero or serrano pepper, seeded

1½ cups (256 g) cooked chickpeas

1 teaspoon toasted sesame oil

½ teaspoon ground cumin

½ teaspoon ground coriander

½ teaspoon ground turmeric

1/16 to 1/8 teaspoon ground cardamom, to taste

1½ cups (258 g) cooked and chilled kamut, farro, or other whole grain

1 tablespoon (15 ml) apple cider vinegar

½ cup (80 g) sulfur-free organic dried Turkish apricots, sliced

1 teaspoon ground sumac, plus extra for garnish

4 thin scallions (1 ounce, or 28 g), thinly sliced

Chopped fresh cilantro and parsley leaves, for garnish

To make the walnuts: Preheat the oven to 325°F (170°C, or gas mark 3). Line a small, rimmed baking sheet with parchment paper. In a small bowl, stir to combine all the ingredients. Toast for 10 minutes, stirring at least once halfway through to make sure the nuts don't burn. Lower the heat to 275°F (140°C, or gas mark 1) and bake for another 8 minutes, or until the nuts aren't sticky anymore. Let cool on the paper. Set aside.

To make the pilaf: Preheat the oven to 400°F (200°C, or gas mark 6). Place the broccoli, salt, garlic, oil, and pepper to a 9-inch (23 cm) baking pan, and fold to combine. Roast in 10-minute increments, stirring after each increment, until the broccoli is tender and lightly browned, about 20 minutes total. Once cooled, mince the garlic and pepper and slightly chop the broccoli.

Place the chickpeas, sesame oil, cumin, coriander, turmeric, and cardamom in a skillet. Sauté on medium heat for 1 minute, to toast the spices. Add the roasted broccoli, garlic, pepper, kamut, vinegar, apricots, sumac, and scallion. Fold to combine, and cook on medium-low heat for another 2 minutes to meld the flavors. Adjust the seasoning if needed. Serve warm or at room temperature with herbs and walnuts. Add a drizzle of pomegranate molasses and a pinch of sumac on top upon serving, if desired.

YIELD: 4 servings

Sweet Potato Berbere Cashew Stew

▶ **NUT**: CASHEW ▶ GLUTEN-FREE POTENTIAL ▶ OIL-FREE ▶ SOY-FREE POTENTIAL

A breeze to make, with awesome results as an added bonus: this one even managed to convince a sweet potato-hater that the orange tuber deserves some love, too. Everyone needs more recipes like this in their repertoire.

Note that berbere spice varies in heat levels, so adjust the quantity accordingly. You can always start with the lower amount if you're unsure, and add a pinch extra at the end.

1 tablespoon (15 ml) fresh lime juice

5 small (scant 18 ounces, or 500 g) sweet potatoes, cut into bite-size pieces

3 carrots (scant 7 ounces, or 180 g), peeled and minced

½ large red onion, chopped

Salt

1 green bell pepper, trimmed and cored, chopped

3 cloves garlic, minced

½ to 1½ teaspoons berbere spice, to taste

½ teaspoon ground cumin

½ teaspoon ground coriander

2 tablespoons (33 g) tomato paste

¼ cup (64 g) toasted cashew butter

1¾ cups (415 ml) low- or no-sodium vegetable broth

Cooked brown rice, to serve

Fresh cilantro leaves

Toasted cashews, coarsely chopped

Place the lime juice, potatoes, carrots, onion, and a couple pinches salt in a large skillet. Stir to combine. Cook on medium-high, stirring occasionally, for 6 minutes. Add the bell pepper, garlic, berbere spice, cumin, coriander, and tomato paste. Cook for another 2 minutes, stirring occasionally; if the vegetables start to stick, add a splash of water and stir to combine.

Add the cashew butter and broth, stirring to combine. Cover with a lid, and lower the heat to simmer until the vegetables are tender, about 30 to 35 minutes. Stir occasionally. Let stand 15 minutes before serving.

Serve on top of rice, garnished with cilantro and cashews.

YIELD: 4 servings

Nutty Gnudi

▶ **NUTS**: ALMOND AND CASHEW

Literally translated from Italian, *gnudi* means nude. Think of these as nude ravioli . . . just the filling! Traditionally these are made with ricotta cheese, herbs and spices, and flour. We've replaced the ricotta with a mixture of ground nuts. These taste great served up with your favorite marinara or pesto, then finished off with a sprinkling of the Pesto Pine Nut Parm-y Sprinkles (page 36).

1¼ cups (150 g) whole wheat pastry flour, or (156 g) all-purpose flour, divided

1 cup (112 g) cashews, soaked at least 4 hours or simmered 15 to 20 minutes, rinsed and drained

½ cup (48 g) almond meal

½ cup (120 ml) olive oil

½ cup (120 ml) unsweetened almond or cashew milk

2 tablespoons (4 g) dried basil

1 tablespoon (8 g) garlic powder

½ teaspoon salt

½ teaspoon black pepper

¼ teaspoon paprika

⅓ cup (40 g) pine nuts

Additional oil for sautéeing

Add 1 cup (120 g) of the flour, cashews, almond meal, oil, milk, herbs, and spices to a food processor. Pulse until a crumble dough is formed. Transfer to a mixing bowl. Fold in the pine nuts. Place the remaining ¼ cup (30 g) flour in a small dish and set aside.

Scoop 1 tablespoon (20 g) of dough into your hand, form it into an oblong ball, and place on a tray or plate. Repeat until all dough is used.

Bring a pot of lightly salted water to a boil. Lightly coat each gnudi in flour and carefully drop into the boiling water, about 6 at a time. Do not overcrowd the pot. Boil for 3 to 4 minutes. Remove from water with a slotted spoon and repeat with remaining gnudis.

Heat a small amount of oil in a frying pan or cast-iron skillet over medium-high heat. Add a few gnudis at a time to the pan, and sauté until a nice golden brown crust is formed. Serve immediately, with your favorite sauce. We happen to love it with the Pistachio Pesto (page 134).

YIELD: 28 pieces

Pea Scramble with Peanut Miso Drizzle

▶ **NUT**: PEANUT ▶ GLUTEN-FREE POTENTIAL ▶ QUICK AND EASY

This saucy scramble can be served on top of finely chopped, cabbage, lightly dressed with carrot pickle brine (page 112) or any other light vinaigrette. It adds a nice touch of color, crunch, and freshness.

If fresh peas aren't available, replace them with the same quantity of frozen peas, thawed before use. Sugar snap peas (trimmed, chopped into bite-size pieces) can also be used.

FOR THE PEANUT MISO DRIZZLE:

¼ cup (64 g) natural crunchy or creamy peanut butter

¼ cup (60 ml) water

2 tablespoons (30 ml) brown rice vinegar, divided

1 tablespoon (18 g) shiro (white) miso

1 teaspoon toasted sesame oil

1 teaspoon agave nectar or other natural liquid sweetener

FOR THE PEA SCRAMBLE:

1½ teaspoons melted coconut oil or peanut oil

1 pound (454 g) super firm tofu, cut into small cubes or crumbled

About 8 dashes liquid smoke

Salt

1 tablespoon (15 ml) tamari

½ cup (65 g) thinly sliced red onion

2 to 3 cloves garlic, thinly sliced

10 ounces (142 g) shelled fresh English peas, cooked just until bright green and crisp

FOR GARNISH:

Scallion, thinly sliced (white and green parts)

Fresh cilantro leaves

Dry-roasted peanuts

To make the Peanut Miso Drizzle: Use an immersion blender or whisk to combine the peanut butter, water, 1 tablespoon (15 ml) vinegar, miso, sesame oil, and agave. Set aside at room temperature while cooking the scramble.

To make the Pea Scramble: Heat the coconut oil in a non-stick skillet on medium-high heat. Add the tofu, splashes of liquid smoke, a healthy couple of pinches of salt, and cook until browned, about 8 minutes. Stir occasionally. Deglaze with the remaining 1 tablespoon (15 ml) vinegar (don't breathe in the unpleasant fumes), and tamari. Add the onion and garlic, and sauté on medium heat for another 2 minutes. Stir the peas into the tofu, and cook until heated through, another 2 minutes.

Serve drizzled with the dressing, garnishing as desired. If you have dressing left, it might thicken when stored in an airtight container in the refrigerator. You can dilute it back to drizzly consistency by stirring 1 tablespoon (15 ml) warm water or broth into it.

YIELD: 3 to 4 servings, ½ cup (120 ml) drizzle

Buffalo Peanut Inside-Out Rolls

▶ NUT: PEANUT ▶ SOY-FREE POTENTIAL

Throw tradition completely out the window with this fun take on buffalo wings made into sushi rolls.

FOR THE RICE:

1 cup (180 g) arborio rice (sushi rice)

2 cups (470 ml) water

1 tablespoon (21 g) agave nectar

1 tablespoon (15 ml) rice vinegar

½ teaspoon salt

FOR THE BUFFALO PEANUTS:

1 tablespoon (15 ml) refined coconut oil, melted

¼ cup (120 ml) your favorite hot sauce (Frank's works well here, as does sriracha)

1 tablespoon (10 g) minced garlic

1 cup (112 g) dry-roasted peanuts

¼ teaspoon black pepper

To make the rice: Place all the ingredients in a rice cooker and follow the instructions on your machine. If you do not have a rice cooker, bring the water and salt to a boil in medium saucepan. Stir in the rice, agave, and vinegar. Return to a boil, reduce to a simmer, cover, and cook until the rice is tender and has absorbed all the liquid, 16 to 18 minutes. Once the rice is cooked, remove from the heat and cool completely.

To make the Buffalo Peanuts: Add the coconut oil, hot sauce, and garlic to a small bowl, and mix together. Add in the peanuts and toss to coat. Heat a large skillet over medium-high heat. Add in the peanuts and sauté until most of the liquid has been absorbed. Remove from the heat and toss with the black pepper. Set aside to cool.

> **Recipe Note**
>
> Not into rolls? Try it as a bowl instead! Simply layer all components in a bowl, drizzle with sauce, and sprinkle with shredded nori sheets, scallion, and dill.

3 sheets of nori, cut in half

5 tablespoons (40 g) sesame seeds

½ cup (120 ml) Creamy Sunflower Buffalo Sauce (page 29)

2 stalks celery, cut into thin julienne strips about 4-inches (10 cm)

1 cup (100 g) chopped scallion

2 tablespoons (7 g) fresh chopped dill

YOU WILL ALSO NEED:

A bamboo sushi rolling mat

A gallon-size resealable plastic bag

Plastic wrap

To assemble the rolls: Place your bamboo mat inside a resealable bag. Place on a flat work surface with the bag opening facing away from you. Place one half-sheet of nori on the edge closest to you. Add ½ cup (3.5 ounces or 100 g) of cooled rice in a single layer about ¼ inch (6 mm) thick to completely cover the nori. Sprinkle liberally with 1 tablespoon (8 g) sesame seeds. Flip over so the rice is face down on the plastic and the nori side is up.

Spread 1 tablespoon (15 ml) of Creamy Sunflower Buffalo Sauce in a thin layer on the nori. Into the center of the nori, layer about 4 pieces of celery, ¼ cup (38 g) of the Buffalo Peanuts, and 2 tablespoons (12 g) scallion.

Carefully roll in the sushi mat to close and create an inside-out roll. Take care to roll as tightly as possible. Open the mat. Cover the entire roll with plastic wrap, then re-roll in the bamboo mat to form the roll. Leave the roll in the plastic wrap, in the refrigerator, until ready to serve.

To serve, carefully unroll from the plastic. Using a very sharp knife, cut off each end of the roll and discard (or eat!). Cut the roll in half, then cut each half into quarters, and finally each quarter into eighths. Carefully remove each piece and arrange on a plate. Drizzle with remaining Creamy Sunflower Buffalo Sauce, and garnish with remaining scallion and dill.

YIELD: 6 rolls (48 pieces)

Pad Tahini

▶ **NUT AND SEED**: PEANUT AND SESAME (TAHINI) ▶ GLUTEN-FREE POTENTIAL

Our spin on pad thai is one of those dishes that tastes even better reheated the next day. Kind of like take-out, with something extra added in: tahini, in this case, which adds extra flavor, protein, and calcium.

1 ounce (28 g) sliced dried shiitake mushrooms, rinsed

2 cups (470 ml) water

¼ cup (64 g) tahini paste

¼ cup (80 g) brown rice syrup or 2 tablespoons plus 2 teaspoons (54 g) agave nectar

2 tablespoons plus 2 teaspoons (40 ml) fresh lime juice

2 tablespoons plus 2 teaspoons (40 ml) tamari, plus extra for serving

2 tablespoons plus 2 teaspoons (40 g) tamarind paste or concentrate

1½ teaspoons peanut oil

¾ cup (120 g) chopped red or white onion

1 red bell pepper, trimmed and chopped

4 cloves garlic, minced, to taste

½ teaspoon red pepper flakes

½ teaspoon coarse kosher salt

½ teaspoon ground turmeric

3 cups (270 g) chopped green cabbage

8 ounces (227 g) brown or regular rice pad thai noodles

1½ teaspoons toasted sesame oil

Garnishes: Thinly sliced scallion, chopped dry-roasted peanuts, roasted sesame seeds, fresh cilantro, and lime wedges

Place the mushrooms in a bowl. Cover with the water. Let stand 10 minutes. Drain, reserving the soaking water. Set aside.

Whisk to combine ½ cup (120 ml) mushroom water, tahini, syrup, juice, tamari, and tamarind in a small saucepan. Heat on medium-high heat, lower the heat and simmer, stirring frequently until just thickened, about 4 minutes.

Heat the peanut oil in a large skillet. Add the onion, and sauté on medium-high heat stirring occasionally until browned, about 6 minutes. Add the mushrooms, bell pepper, and garlic, and sauté until the pepper just starts to soften. Add the pepper flakes, salt, and turmeric. Stir to toast for 1 minute. Add the cabbage, and sauté until softened but still crisp, about 4 minutes.

In the meantime, bring to a boil the last of the mushroom water combined with enough water to generously cover the noodles. Carefully remove from the heat, add the noodles, and soak until al dente, following the instructions on the package. Drain, then stir the sesame oil into the noodles.

Stir the noodles and as much sauce as desired into the vegetables, and simmer to meld the flavors, about 4 minutes. Serve with garnishes and extra tamari, if desired. If you have leftovers of the sauce, use them to moisten leftovers.

YIELD: 4 to 6 servings

Basic Chickpea Cashew Omelet

▶ **NUT**: CASHEW ▶ GLUTEN-FREE POTENTIAL ▶ QUICK AND EASY

The following omelet makes quite an impression cut into strips in our Thai Fried Wild Rice (page 97), where it adds a healthy boost of protein. It tastes great as a solo performer as well, or served with Cheesy Almond Gravy (page 31). We often add a handful of minced fresh herbs and veggies (such as onions, bell peppers, and mushrooms) to the batter before cooking the omelet. No need to bother cutting into strips in this case, unless you want to use it as an addition to salads.

½ cup (120 ml) unsweetened plain cashew or almond milk

1½ teaspoons brown rice vinegar

1½ teaspoons fresh lime juice

1 teaspoon light miso

1 teaspoon grapeseed oil

¼ cup plus 2 tablespoons (45 g) garbanzo fava bean flour or chickpea flour, sifted

2 tablespoons (15 g) cashew or almond meal

1 tablespoon (8 g) nutritional yeast

¼ teaspoon coarse kosher salt

¼ teaspoon ground turmeric

Nonstick cooking spray or oil spray

Whisk all the ingredients, except cooking spray, in a medium glass bowl. Set aside for 5 minutes. Heat a large, nonstick pan on medium-high heat. Lower the heat to medium. Lightly coat the pan with cooking spray or oil spray once hot, away from the heat.

Pour the batter into the pan: it should spread itself to an 8-inch (20 cm) circle. Let cook for about 6 minutes. Carefully lift the edges to make sure it is golden brown, which means it can be flipped.

Carefully flip with a large spatula, and let cook for another 6 minutes, or until golden brown.

If using in the Thai Fried Wild Rice (page 97), transfer to a cooling rack before cutting into small strips (about 1 inch or 2.5 cm in length, ¼ inch or 6 mm in thickness) with a sharp knife. This can be done ahead of time and stored in an airtight container in the refrigerator until ready to use, up to 1 day ahead. (Chilling the omelet will make for easier cutting.) Note that you can also make 2 smaller, 4-inch (10 cm) omelets, cooking them in two separate batches.

If using as is and not cut into strips, serve immediately.

YIELD: 1 omelet

Thai Fried Wild Rice with Sriracha Lime Cashews

▶ **NUT**: CASHEW ▶ GLUTEN-FREE POTENTIAL

Cashews can do no wrong! That's our motto. We love the crunchy, spicy attitude they bring to this colorful, flavorful plate. If you're looking for a change, the same quantity (⅔ cup [112 g]) of raw Brazil nuts is wonderful too, coarsely chopped once cooled.

FOR THE CASHEWS:

⅔ cup (93 g) raw whole cashews

1½ teaspoons sriracha sauce

1½ teaspoons fresh lime juice

½ teaspoon agave nectar

Couple generous pinches coarse kosher salt

FOR THE FRIED RICE:

1 recipe Basic Chickpea Cashew Omelet (page 96), prepared and chilled

1 tablespoon (15 ml) peanut oil or melted coconut oil

¼ cup (40 g) minced shallot or red onion

1 generous cup (90 g) chopped red cabbage

2 cloves garlic, minced

½ jalapeño or other hot pepper, seeded and minced, to taste

1½ cups (190 g) cooked and cooled wild rice

2 teaspoons (10 ml) toasted sesame oil

1 cup (130 g) carrot pickles (page 112)

1 tablespoon (15 ml) brine from carrot pickles (page 112), to taste

1 teaspoon tamari, to taste

⅓ cup (27 g) thinly sliced scallion

Fresh cilantro leaves, for garnish

Thin English cucumber slices, for garnish

To make the cashews: Preheat the oven to 325°F (170°C, or gas mark 3). Line a small, rimmed baking sheet with parchment paper. In a small bowl, stir to combine all the ingredients. Roast for 10 to 15 minutes, until the nuts are fragrant and dry, checking and stirring every 5 minutes to make sure the nuts don't burn. Let cool on the paper, separating once cooled. Set aside.

To make the fried rice: Cut the chilled omelet into 1-inch (2.5 cm) strips with a sharp knife. Set aside. Heat the oil in a large wok or skillet. Add the shallot and cook on medium-high heat until softened, about 3 minutes. Add the cabbage, garlic, and pepper. Sauté for about 2 minutes; the cabbage should remain crisp. Add the rice and cook until heated through, about 2 minutes. Transfer the mixture to a large bowl.

Wipe the sides of the wok if there were spills and return to medium heat. Heat the sesame oil, and add the omelet strips. Sauté until heated through and slightly browned, about 3 minutes.

Add the carrot pickles, brine, and tamari to taste to the rice bowl, folding with a rubber spatula to combine. Serve immediately with cashews, scallion, cilantro, and cucumber.

YIELD: 3 to 4 servings

Cashew-Crusted Grilled Cheese with Charred Apples

▶ **NUT**: CASHEW ▶ SOY-FREE POTENTIAL ▶ QUICK AND EASY

This grown-up grilled cheese pairs tart green apples with a savory spread, and sandwiches it all in between toasty bread with a cashew crust.

FOR THE BALSAMIC THYME SPREAD:

⅓ cup (75 g) Simple Cashew Mayo (page 27), or store-bought vegan mayo

1 tablespoon (15 g) whole-grain mustard (spicy mustard is great here)

1 tablespoon (15 ml) balsamic vinegar

¼ teaspoon dried thyme

FOR THE GRILLED CHEESE:

8 slices of hearty bread

2 green apples, skin on, thinly sliced

½ cup (56 g) finely ground cashews

½ teaspoon dill

¼ teaspoon garlic powder

¼ teaspoon onion powder

¼ teaspoon paprika

8 slices of bread

½ cup (112 g) Simple Cashew Mayo (page 27), or store-bought vegan mayo

½ cup (128 g) cashew butter

4 slices of Simple Nutty Cheese (page 40), or your favorite store-bought vegan cheese

1 cup (30 g) greens, such as arugula, mixed baby greens, spinach, or watercress

To make the Balsamic Thyme Spread: Mix all the ingredients together and set aside.

To make the grilled cheese: Preheat a grill pan over medium heat. Arrange the apple slices in a single layer in the pan, and grill until the sugars in the apple caramelize and char, about 5 minutes per side. Remove from the pan and set aside.

In a small bowl, mix together the ground cashews, dill, garlic powder, onion powder, and paprika. Set aside. Spread 1 tablespoon (16 g) cashew butter on one side of each of the slices of bread. Layer slices of charred apple, cheese, Balsamic Thyme Spread, and greens on 4 of the slices of bread, then top with remaining 4 slices of bread.

Preheat a frying pan or griddle over medium heat. You can also use a panini press for this! Spread one tablespoon (14 g) of mayo on the top slice of bread on each of the sandwiches. Sprinkle liberally with the ground cashew mixture. Place the sandwich crusted-bread side down on the pan. As the sandwich is cooking, spread the other side of the sandwich (now facing up) with 1 tablespoon (14 g) of mayo and sprinkle with the remaining cashew mixture.

Carefully flip the sandwich when golden brown and crispy. Cover the entire sandwich with a stainless-steel mixing bowl, or handled pot, to trap the heat inside and melt the cheese. Carefully remove the bowl or pot, when golden brown and crispy. Remove from the pan and serve.

YIELD: 4 sandwiches

This Burger Is Nuts!

▶ **NUTS AND SEEDS**: CASHEW, PECAN, WALNUT, AND SUNFLOWER SEED

Protein-packed and full of earthy nutty flavor, this burger stands up well to many types of cuisine. So feel free to dress it up as you wish, or in other words . . . go nuts!

2 tablespoons (30 ml) olive oil, plus more for frying (optional)

8 ounces (227 g) mushrooms, sliced or chopped

3 cloves garlic, minced

¾ cup (180 ml) vegetable broth

1 cup (100 g) prepared brown rice

¼ cup (28 g) raw cashews, chopped

¼ cup (32 g) sunflower seeds

¼ cup (27 g) pecans, chopped

¼ cup (30 g) walnuts, chopped

¼ cup (30 g) nutritional yeast

½ cup (72 g) vital wheat gluten

1 tablespoon (8 g) ground mustard

1 tablespoon (8 g) onion powder

Salt and pepper

In a heavy-bottom skillet, heat the oil and sauté the mushrooms and garlic for 5 to 7 minutes, or until fragrant and translucent. Add the vegetable broth and bring to a simmer. Add the rice, nuts, and seeds. Mix well, cover, and remove from the heat. Let sit for 10 minutes.

When cool enough to handle, add the nutritional yeast, gluten, ground mustard, and onion powder. Salt and pepper to taste, and mix well using your hands. Place in the fridge to cool for about 20 minutes. This will help the dough stiffen up a bit. Form into 4 to 8 patties, depending on preference.

Preheat the oven to 350°F (180°C, or gas mark 4). Line a baking sheet with parchment or a reusable silicone baking mat. Arrange the patties on the mat, and bake for 25 minutes. Flip and bake an additional 15 minutes. Alternatively, you can panfry these burgers in a bit of oil for 4 to 5 minutes per side until crispy and golden.

YIELD: 4 patties (½ pound, or 227 g) or 8 patties (¼ pound, or 114 g)

Texas Hold 'Ems (Savory BBQ Pecans)

▶ **NUT**: PECAN

If Texas is known for one thing, it's BBQ. But did you know Texas is also known for its pecans? Here we smother and simmer pecans in a sassy barbecue sauce and then stuff them into a handhold (a pita, tortilla, French roll, or even tacos) along with some chopped salad. As written, this recipe makes a bunch, but it keeps well in the fridge. If you make a big batch of the pecans, you can definitely use them in all sorts of ways.

FOR THE BARBECUE PECANS:

2 tablespoons (30 ml) olive oil

1 cup (160 g) diced red onion

2 tablespoons (20 g) minced garlic

1½ cups (366 g) tomato sauce

1 cup (235 ml) pineapple juice

¼ cup (60 ml) pure maple syrup

2 to 3 tablespoons (30 to 45 ml) sriracha sauce, to taste

2 tablespoons (44 g) molasses

2 tablespoons (30 ml) vegan Worcestershire sauce

¼ teaspoon liquid smoke

4 cups (396 g) pecans, soaked overnight and drained (see Note)

Salt and pepper

To make the Barbecue Pecans: Add the olive oil to the bottom of a pan and heat over medium heat. Add the diced onion and sauté until fragrant and translucent and the edges are browned, about 5 to 8 minutes. Add the garlic and continue to sauté 2 to 3 more minutes. Add in the remaining ingredients, except the pecans, salt, and pepper. Stir to combine. Bring to a simmer, add in the pecans, stir to combine, cover, reduce the heat to medium-low. Simmer for 20 minutes, returning to stir halfway through.

Recipe Note

This recipe will work out just fine if you don't soak your pecans, but soaking them makes them even chewier (desirable in this recipe).

FOR THE ALMOND BUTTERMILK
RANCH DRESSING:

¾ cup (180 ml) unsweetened
almond milk

2 teaspoons (10 ml) fresh lemon juice

2 teaspoons (10 ml) apple cider vinegar

½ cup (120 ml) mild-flavored
vegetable oil

1 tablespoon (15 g) Dijon mustard

2 teaspoons (3 g) onion powder

1 teaspoon garlic powder

1 teaspoon dried dill, or 1 tablespoon
(4 g) fresh

¼ to ½ teaspoon salt, to taste

½ teaspoon xanthan gum

FOR THE CHOPPED SALAD:

1 pound (454 g) romaine lettuce,
chopped into small pieces

1 medium red onion (about 6 ounces,
or 170 g) peeled and finely diced

1 bunch (2 ounces, or 56 g) cilantro,
chopped

FOR THE HANDHOLDS:

Bread, rolls, pita, or tortillas

To make the Almond Buttermilk Ranch Dressing: Add the
almond milk, lemon juice, and vinegar to your blender. (If
you have an immersion blender this works perfectly here.)
Let the mixture sit for a few minutes. It will curdle and
become like buttermilk. Add in the remaining ingredients,
and blend until combined and thickened. Refrigerate until
ready to use.

To make the chopped salad: In a large mixing bowl, toss
together the romaine, onion, and cilantro. Toss with dressing. If preparing in advance, do not toss with dressing
until ready to serve. Assemble your handholds by layering
the chopped salad and Barbecue Pecans in the handheld
delivery method of your choice.

YIELD: 8 servings of pecans and salad, and 1½ cups (455 ml)
dressing

Tempeh Nut Butter Sandwiches

▶ NUT: CASHEW OR OTHER ▶ OIL-FREE POTENTIAL

Cashew butter is the perfect addition to these attractive sandwiches because of its richness and great flavor. It also helps tame the chipotle pepper heat.

FOR THE TEMPEH:

1½ tablespoons (23 ml) adobo sauce

1 to 1½ chipotle peppers in adobo sauce, minced, to taste

1½ tablespoons (23 ml) fresh lime juice

1½ tablespoons (30 g) agave nectar

¾ teaspoon ground cumin

¾ teaspoon coarse kosher salt

8 ounces (227 g) tempeh, cut in half widthwise, then lengthwise, each quarter widthwise again, halved in thickness to create 16 small rectangular patties

FOR THE VEGGIES AND SANDWICHES:

1½ tablespoons (23 ml) adobo sauce

1½ tablespoons (23 ml) fresh lime juice

⅜ teaspoon ground cumin

⅜ teaspoon coarse kosher salt, to taste

1 red bell pepper, cut into ½-inch (1.3 cm) rings and cored

1 medium white or yellow onion, cut into ⅓-inch (9 mm) rings

Olive oil, for grilling (optional)

½ cup (128 g) roasted cashew butter or other nut or seed butter

8 slices of vegan whole-grain sandwich bread, lightly toasted

Fresh cilantro leaves

Avocado slices (optional)

To make the tempeh: In a 9-inch (23 cm) square baking pan, whisk to combine all the ingredients except the tempeh. Place the tempeh in the marinade, cover, and marinate for at least 1 hour in the refrigerator, flipping once halfway through. (See directions below to marinate the veggies at the same time as the tempeh.)

Preheat the oven to 375°F (190°C, or gas mark 5). Line a large baking sheet with parchment paper. Bake the tempeh for 8 minutes on each side, basting it with remaining marinade as you flip. Remove from the oven and place on a cooling rack. Alternatively, you can choose to only grill the tempeh. The grilling time will be longer if not previously baked, but it will spare you from having to use the oven. We like combining baking and grilling for great texture and flavor.

To make the veggies and sandwiches: In a large bowl, whisk to combine the sauce, juice, cumin, and salt. Add the bell pepper and onion, tossing to coat. Marinate for at least 1 hour in the refrigerator.

Heat a grill pan or an actual grill. Lightly brush with oil if your grill needs it, but this shouldn't be necessary. Grill the vegetables, basting with the leftover veggie marinade if needed, until crisp tender and grill marks appear. Timing will vary, but approximately 4 minutes on each side. If desired, grill the tempeh as well, basting it with leftover veggie marinade.

Spread 1 tablespoon (16 g) cashew butter on each bread slice, or enough to cover. Top 4 of the buttered bread slices with 4 tempeh slices each. Top with 2 pepper rings, and as much onion as desired. Top with cilantro to taste, and avocado if desired. Finally, top with the 4 remaining buttered bread slices, and cut in half. Serve immediately.

YIELD: 4 sandwiches

Recipe Notes

- If you find the tempeh you use has a bitter taste, submerge the unprepared block of tempeh in water and simmer it for 20 minutes. Drain well, allow to cool a moment, then proceed with the recipe as noted.

- Natural nut butters must be stored in the refrigerator in order to keep them from becoming rancid. The downside to this is that it can make spreading on bread a little difficult. The answer lies in the toasting: Don't allow the warm bread to cool down before applying the nut butter. Place the desired amount of nut butter on the slice, and wait just a beat for the residual heat to soften the nut butter and avoid a torn-up mess.

- This recipe has gluten-free potential, provided you make sure the brand of chipotle peppers in adobo sauce is free of gluten. According to the manufacturer, La Costena brand's chipotle peppers are gluten-free but it's safest to double check before use. When in doubt, you can always make your own by searching for recipes online. The other obvious change needed to make this recipe gluten-free is of course to use a bread that is free of gluten.

- Fancy some tacos instead of sandwiches? Simply replace the bread with eight 6-inch (15 cm) corn tortillas, heated to make pliable. Apply enough nut butter to cover the surface, add filling (chopped in smaller bites or left as is), fold, and eat!

Cashew Avocado Toast with Pistachio Dukkah

▶ **NUTS AND SEEDS**: CASHEW OR ALMOND, PISTACHIO, AND SESAME ▶ GLUTEN-FREE POTENTIAL ▶ OIL-FREE ▶ SOY-FREE POTENTIAL ▶ QUICK AND EASY

If you spend way too much time on the internet like we do, you can't not have noticed how popular avocado toast has become in recent years. We paired our version with roasted cashew butter and a generous dusting of pistachio dukkah. The more nuts and seeds, the merrier: that's the number one rule of this book—and therefore in real life as well.

4 slices of vegan whole-grain bread

2 small avocados, pitted, peeled, and coarsely mashed

Fresh lemon juice, as needed

¼ cup (64 g) roasted crunchy or creamy cashew or almond butter, as needed

1 tomato, thinly sliced

4 razor-thin slices of red onion

1 recipe Pistachio Dukkah (page 34)

Begin by toasting your bread. While the bread is toasting, coarsely mash the avocados in a small bowl with a few drops of lemon juice.

When the bread is toasted, apply a thin layer of cashew butter on each slice. Top each with an even layer of a quarter of the mashed avocado, 2 tomato slices, a slice of onion, and as much dukkah as will fit without falling off as you eat. Serve immediately.

YIELD: 4 servings

Recipe Note

If you don't particularly care for raw onion, you can replace it with a small handful of your favorite kind of super fresh sprouts (place them under the avocado to avoid messy eats), scallion, or even some thinly sliced radish.

The Monte Cristina

▶ **NUT**: PEANUT

A Monte Cristo sandwich is two slices of French toast filled with fried ham and cheese. It is then sprinkled with powdered sugar and served with fruit preserves. This is Cristo's Latina cousin, Cristina. She's spicy and sweet, with a touch of sass.

FOR THE BLACKENED TOFU:

½ teaspoon onion powder

½ teaspoon garlic powder

½ teaspoon ground turmeric

¼ teaspoon black salt (kala namak)

¼ teaspoon paprika

¼ teaspoon chipotle powder

Salt and pepper

1 block (1 pound, or 454 g) extra or super firm tofu (I love to use smoked tofu for this recipe), drained and pressed, then cut into 8 thin squares

FOR THE SPICY FRENCH TOAST:

8 slices of bread (this is a great way to use up stale bread)

½ cup (120 ml) prepared Peanut Chipotle Ranch Dressing (page 28)

FOR THE SANDWICH:

½ cup (128 g) peanut butter

1 cup (30 g) mixed baby greens, tightly packed

16 slices of cucumber

½ cup (120 ml) pure maple syrup

¼ cup (28 g) chopped peanuts

¼ cup (30 g) nutritional yeast

To make the tofu: Add the spices to a resealable plastic bag or a shallow dish with a lid. Shake to mix. Add the tofu and shake to coat.

To cook the tofu, you can panfry in a bit of oil, or bake at 375°F (190°C, or gas mark 5) for about 15 minutes per side, or until blackened . . . but we love to use a waffle maker to cook the tofu so that it's crisp and blackened on the outside, but soft, moist, and chewy on the inside. To do this, spray nonstick spray on the waffle iron, then place one layer of tofu inside and lock closed. It cooks perfectly, and you won't have to heat up the entire oven to make it.

To make the spicy French toast: Spread 1 tablespoon (15 ml) of the Chipotle Peanut Ranch Dressing on each side of the 8 pieces of bread. Cook on a flat pan or griddle over medium-high heat until browned. Flip and repeat on the other side. Repeat with all 8 slices.

To assemble the sandwich: Spread 1 tablespoon (16 g) of peanut butter on one side of each of the pieces of French toast.

Layer ¼ cup (7 g) mixed baby greens, 2 squares of blackened tofu, and 4 slices of cucumber to 4 slices of French toast. Then top with remaining 4 slices.

Cut in half, if desired, and plate. Drizzle each sandwich with 2 tablespoons (30 ml) of maple syrup, then sprinkle with 1 tablespoon (7 g) each of chopped peanuts and nutritional yeast. We suggest eating this bad girl with a fork, as she tends to get a little messy!

YIELD: 4 sandwiches

Sesame Walnut Bean Ball Banh Mi

▶ NUTS AND SEEDS: WALNUT, ALMOND, SESAME, AND FLAX ▶ GLUTEN-FREE POTENTIAL

This twist on a banh mi is as beautiful as it is delicious.

FOR THE QUICK PICKLED VEGETABLES:

½ cup (54 g) shredded carrots

½ cup (8 g) chopped cilantro

½ cup (50 g) chopped scallion

10 radishes, thinly sliced

3 stalks celery, chopped

1 cucumber, half-moon slices

3 cups (705 ml) water

⅓ cup (80 ml) white vinegar

2 tablespoons (36 g) salt

FOR THE SESAME WALNUT BEAN BALLS:

2 cups (240 g) walnut pieces

1 can (15 ounces, or g) chickpeas, with the liquid

1 cup (30 g) packed baby spinach leaves

½ cup (80 g) diced yellow onion

2 tablespoons (30 ml) sesame oil

½ teaspoon salt

¼ cup (30 g) nutritional yeast

¼ cup (26 g) ground flaxseed

¼ cup (24 g) almond flour

¼ cup (30 g) oat flour

½ cup (64 g) sesame seeds

FOR THE SESAME SRIRACHA SAUCE:

1 cup (224 g) Simple Cashew Mayo (page 27) (or any vegan mayo)

2 tablespoons (30 ml) sesame oil

2 tablespoons (30 ml) sriracha sauce

FOR THE SANDWICHES:

French baguettes, sliced to desired size

¼ cup chopped cilantro, for garnish

To make the Quick Pickled Vegetables: Add all the vegetables, water, vinegar, and salt to a gallon-size resealable plastic bag or a shallow dish with a lid. Shake to combine, then remove as much of the air out of the bag as possible. Store in the refrigerator until ready to use.

Preheat the oven to 350°F (180°C, or gas mark 4). Have ready a baking sheet lined with parchment or a reusable baking mat.

To make the Sesame Walnut Bean Balls: Add the walnut pieces, chickpeas with liquid, spinach, onion, oil, and salt to a food processor. Purée until well combined but still a little chunky.

Transfer to a bowl. Stir in the nutritional yeast, flaxseed, almond flour, and oat flour. Your mixture should be thick, but not dry, and able to hold a ball shape when formed. If your mixture is still too wet, add in a little more flour. If it is too dry, add in a little water 1 teaspoon at a time.

Place the sesame seeds in a shallow dish. Form a heaping tablespoon (30 g) of mixture into a ball and roll in the seeds to coat. Place on the baking sheet and repeat with remaining mixture. You should get about 24 balls out of the mixture. Bake for 30 minutes, checking after 20 minutes to make sure the sesame seeds aren't burning.

To make the sauce: While balls are baking, make the sauce. Stir the mayo together with sesame oil and sriracha until smooth. If you have a squeeze bottle, put the sauce in that, as it makes for pretty drizzles (you can also cut the corner off of a plastic bag). Refrigerate until ready to use.

To assemble the sandwiches: Cut the baguette open horizontally, leaving one edge attached (like a hot dog bun). Add the desired amount of balls to the baguette then top with quick pickled veg, then drizzle liberally with sauce. Top with a garnish of chopped cilantro, if desired.

YIELD: 24 balls, or enough to fill 4 to 8 sandwiches

Thai Peanut Pizza

▶ **NUTS**: PEANUT AND ALMOND

This pizza is bursting with flavor from the savory peanut sauce base to the fresh herb flavor from the basil and cilantro. The celery and toasted almonds give it a nice crunch, and the avocado makes an excellent creamy stand-in for cheese. The Cilantro Crema makes more than you will need for the pizza alone, but it also works as a great salad dressing. The Crema is also the garnish for the Potato Peanut Soup (page 118).

FOR THE CILANTRO CREMA:

1 cup (224 g) Simple Cashew Mayo (page 27), or any store-bought vegan mayo

1 bunch (3 ounces, or 85 g) cilantro (reserve ¼ cup (4 g) chopped leaves for use in the pizza below)

3 tablespoons (45 ml) rice vinegar

1 tablespoon (10 g) minced garlic

1 teaspoon sesame oil

FOR THE PIZZA:

1 premade pizza dough, thawed according to package instructions

½ cup (120 ml) Thai Peanut Sauce (page 29)

1 cup (70 g) shredded green or purple cabbage

1 cup (101 g) chopped celery

1 cup (108 g) shredded carrots

20 leaves fresh basil, sliced chiffonade

½ cup (50 g) chopped fresh chives or scallion

¼ cup (4 g) reserved cilantro chopped leaves

1 ripe avocado, sliced

1 cup (108 g) Ginger Soy Wasabi Toasted Almonds (page 83)

1 teaspoon sesame seeds (black or white, or both!)

Red chili flakes, to taste

To make the Cilantro Crema: Add all the ingredients to a blender (you can add the stems from the cilantro, they are packed with flavor!). Purée until smooth. Store in an airtight container or a squeeze bottle, in the refrigerator until ready to use.

To make the pizza: Preheat the oven to 475°F (246°C, or gas mark 9). Have ready a baking sheet lightly floured or lined with parchment. If you have a pizza stone, preheat it and have it ready.

Stretch your pizza to a 9 x 12-inch (23 x 30 cm) rectangle and place it on the pan. (Or stretch to fit your pan.) Spread the peanut sauce all over the dough. Sprinkle on the cabbage, celery, and carrots evenly over the pizza. Bake for 12 to 15 minutes, or until crust is golden brown.

Remove from the oven and top with basil, chives or scallion, and cilantro. Evenly space the avocado slices, then drizzle the entire pizza with Cilantro Crema. Sprinkle on the Ginger Soy Wasabi Almonds, sesame seeds, and the desired amount of red chili flakes. Slice and serve.

YIELD: 1 pizza

Hawaiian Macadamia Tacos

▶ **NUT**: MACADAMIA ▶ GLUTEN-FREE POTENTIAL ▶ SOY-FREE POTENTIAL

If you aren't a big fan of coconut, you can choose to skip the sauce altogether because the salsa brings a bold enough flavor to these tasty tacos.

FOR THE SALSA:

1 cup (180 g) fresh pineapple in small chunks, chopped

1 small to medium jalapeño or serrano pepper (seeded or not), minced, to taste

¼ cup plus 2½ tablespoons (65 g) chopped red onion

1 tablespoon (15 ml) fresh lime juice

Coarse kosher salt

FOR THE SAUCE:

¼ cup (60 g) coconut butter (see Recipe Note)

¼ cup (60 ml) water

Few grates of lime zest, to taste

8 teaspoons (40 ml) fresh lime juice

4 teaspoons (20 ml) toasted sesame oil

2 cloves garlic, grated or pressed

Coarse kosher salt

FOR THE TACOS:

8 freshly cooked or softened 6-inch (15 cm) corn tortillas

1 cup (185 g) cooked quinoa (still warm or chilled)

Finely chopped red cabbage

¾ cup (84 g) dry-roasted macadamia nuts, coarsely chopped (lightly salted is acceptable)

Fresh cilantro leaves, to taste

To make the salsa: Place all the ingredients in a small bowl. Stir to combine. Cover and chill for 1 hour in the refrigerator.

To make the sauce: Prepare when ready to eat by placing all the ingredients in a small bowl, and whisk to combine. Do not refrigerate as the sauce will harden.

To assemble the tacos: In the length of the center of each tortilla, place 2 tablespoons (24 g) quinoa, a pinch of cabbage, 2 tablespoons (30 g) salsa, a drizzle of sauce, 1 tablespoon (7 g) chopped nuts, and cilantro. Serve immediately.

YIELD: 8 tacos, 1 cup (240 g) salsa, scant 1 cup (220 ml) sauce

Recipe Note

To make coconut butter: Use a blender or food processor to turn a bag of unsweetened shredded coconut into butter; this might take up to 10 minutes depending on the machine. Stop occasionally to scrape the sides of the machine with a rubber spatula and to prevent overheating. Note that it's unlikely the butter will become completely smooth. Store in airtight jar at room temperature to keep from hardening.

Vietnamese Peanut Tacos

▶ **NUT**: PEANUT ▶ GLUTEN-FREE POTENTIAL ▶ OIL-FREE ▶ SOY-FREE POTENTIAL

Like all tacos, a multitude of components makes for an outstanding—and quite nutritious in this case—outcome. Prepare the pickles and tempeh ahead of time, and you'll find that you can get these colorful wonders on the table rather quickly.

FOR THE CARROT PICKLES:

4 medium carrots, cut in 2-inch (5 cm) pieces widthwise, thinly sliced lengthwise (use a mandoline slicer)

1 teaspoon sambal oelek

2 large cloves garlic, grated or pressed

¼ cup (60 ml) brown rice vinegar

¼ cup (60 ml) seasoned rice vinegar

¼ cup (60 ml) water

2 teaspoons (6 g) coarse kosher salt

2 teaspoons (8 g) coconut sugar or other sugar

½ teaspoon ginger powder

FOR THE TEMPEH:

2 tablespoons (30 ml) tamari

1 tablespoon (15 ml) sriracha sauce

1 tablespoon (20 g) agave nectar or brown rice syrup

1 teaspoon ume plum vinegar

2 cloves garlic, grated or pressed

8 ounces (227 g) tempeh, cut in half widthwise, then lengthwise, then each quarter widthwise again, and halved in thickness to create 16 thin, small, rectangular patties

To make the carrot pickles: Place the carrots, sambal oelek, and garlic in a heat-resistant bowl or container. Place the vinegars and water in a non-reactive saucepan. Bring to a boil, and remove from the heat. Don't breathe in the vinegar fumes: it isn't dangerous, just unpleasant. Stir the salt, sugar, and ginger into the vinegar mixture to dissolve the sugar. Pour this mixture on top of the carrots, and stir to combine. The brine will not fully cover the carrots at first, but it will as they soften. Cover with a lid or plastic wrap, and set aside to cool to room temperature, stirring once or twice. Refrigerate for 24 hours before use. Store in the refrigerator for up to 1 week. (Do not discard the brine, it will be used in other recipes!)

To make the tempeh: In a 9-inch (23 cm) square baking pan, whisk to combine the tamari, sriracha, agave, vinegar, and garlic. Place the tempeh in the marinade, cover, and allow to marinate for at least 1 hour in the refrigerator, flipping once halfway through.

Preheat the oven to 375°F (190°C, or gas mark 5). Line a large baking sheet with parchment paper. Bake the tempeh for 8 minutes on each side. Remove from the oven, place on a cooling rack, and let cool to room temperature. Once cooled, chop into bite-size pieces.

FOR THE TACOS:

8 freshly cooked or softened 6-inch (15 cm) corn tortillas

2 scant cups (120 g) finely chopped red cabbage

24 3-inch (7.5 cm) long thin English cucumber slices

Double recipe Almond Lime Sauce (page 124, made with natural peanut butter)

Sriracha sauce

Thinly sliced scallion

Fresh cilantro leaves

½ cup (56 g) unsalted dry-roasted peanuts, coarsely chopped

To assemble the tacos: Place a scant ¼ cup (15 g) cabbage in the length of the center of a tortilla. (Don't be too generous with each component, or the tacos will be overstuffed and be a mess to eat.) Top with 4 pickled carrots (remove excess pickling liquid from carrots before adding). Top with 3 cucumber slices. Top with the equivalent of 2 tempeh slices. Top with Almond Lime Sauce and a drizzle of sriracha sauce, to taste. Top with sliced scallion and cilantro leaves to taste, and 1 tablespoon (7 g) chopped peanuts. Serve immediately.

YIELD: 8 tacos

Walnut, Arugula, and Grape Tacos

▶ **NUTS**: WALNUT AND PEANUT ▶ GLUTEN-FREE POTENTIAL
▶ OIL-FREE POTENTIAL ▶ QUICK AND EASY

These tacos are a breeze to whip up—a few whizzes in the food processor and *voilà*, walnut taco meat.

FOR THE WALNUT TACO MEAT:

2 cups (240 g) walnut pieces

2 tablespoons (30 ml) red wine vinegar

2 tablespoons (30 ml) tequila

2 tablespoons (30 ml) fresh lime juice

1 chipotle in adobo sauce

1 tablespoon (10 g) minced garlic

1 tablespoon (8 g) chili powder

1 tablespoon (8 g) onion powder

1 tablespoon (7 g) paprika

½ teaspoon dried oregano

½ teaspoon black pepper

½ teaspoon ground cumin

Salt (optional)

FOR THE TACOS:

24 small corn tortillas

2 cups (40 g) arugula or any other bitter leafy green

½ cup (80 g) diced red or white onion

½ cup (75 g) cherry tomatoes, halved

½ cup (76 g) red or green grapes, halved

½ cup (120 ml) Peanut Chipotle Ranch Dressing (page 28)

½ cup (8 g) chopped cilantro, for garnish

To make the Walnut Taco Meat: Add all the ingredients to a food processor. Pulse until combined and mashed. You don't want a paste, you want a few bigger pieces left so it is chunky and has a meaty texture with a bit of bite. It can be eaten as is, or heated to desired temperature before serving.

To assemble the tacos: First toast the tortillas in a dry pan and keep warm in a tortilla warmer (or a bowl with a towel laid over it). To serve, add a layer of arugula on top of 2 (stacked) tortillas followed by the Walnut Taco Meat, diced onions, cherry tomatoes, and grapes. Drizzle with Peanut Chipotle Ranch Dressing and garnish with cilantro. Repeat with the remaining tacos.

YIELD: 12 street style–size tacos

5

SUBSTANTIAL SOUPS, SIDES, AND SALADS

The Nut-So-Secret Way to Create Nourishing Small Meals or Sides

In the mood for smaller meals for yourself? Are you looking for a variety of appetizers to show off your cooking skills to hungry guests? Perhaps you're simply craving a warm, comforting bowl of soup or a refreshing plateful of greens, depending on the season. It's a fortunate coincidence because there's no limit to the versatility of nuts and seeds. They add a healthy bunch of nutritional value to the plate (or bowl!), and they also beautifully showcase their inimitable flavor and irresistible crunch. We're all smitten here.

Sesame Za'atar Pepper Soup with Roasted Pepitas

▶ **SEEDS**: SESAME (TAHINI) AND PEPITA ▶ GLUTEN-FREE POTENTIAL
▶ SOY-FREE POTENTIAL

Enjoy this colorful soup with crunchy tortilla chips or pita chips on the side: they also help tame the spiciness. If you like milder foods, either halve the amount of jalapeño or nix it completely. Make the most out of your oven roasting time: roast the peppers needed here alongside those for pages 37 and 39. The roasting can also be done ahead of time; refrigerate the cooled peppers in an airtight container.

1 large red bell pepper

1 poblano pepper

1 small jalapeño pepper

1 generous cup (157 g) frozen corn

3 tablespoons (48 g) tahini paste

3 tablespoons (45 ml) water

2¾ cups (650 ml) vegetable broth

1½ teaspoons grapeseed oil

Scant ¾ cup (110 g) diced red onion

1 tablespoon (10 g) za'atar blend
(page 17)

2 teaspoons (11 g) tomato paste

2 cloves garlic, minced

1 tablespoon (15 ml) fresh lemon juice

½ cup (110 g) drained fire-roasted diced tomatoes or any diced tomato

FOR GARNISH:

Dry-roasted pepitas

Fresh cilantro leaves

Tortilla chips or pita chips

Preheat the oven to 425°F (220°C, or gas mark 7). Place the whole peppers on a medium rimmed baking sheet. Roast until soft and slightly charred, about 25 minutes. Check every 10 minutes to make sure the peppers don't burn, and flip to char both sides.

At the same time, place the frozen corn in an 8-inch (20 cm) square baking pan. Roast until lightly browned, about 25 minutes, stirring once halfway through.

While the peppers and corn are roasting, whisk the tahini with the water in a small bowl. Whisk into the broth.

When the peppers are done, place them in a glass bowl fitted with a lid to steam for about 10 minutes. Once cool enough to handle, peel the peppers, and discard their seeds and core. Mince the jalapeño, and chop the other peppers into bite-size pieces.

Place the oil and onion in a large pot. Sauté on medium-high heat until quite fragrant and lightly browned, about 4 minutes. Lower the heat to medium, and add the za'atar, tomato paste, and garlic, cooking for about 30 seconds. Deglaze with the lemon juice. Add the roasted peppers and corn, broth, and tomatoes. Bring to a boil, lower the heat, and simmer uncovered 15 minutes, until slightly thickened, stirring occasionally. Serve topped with garnishes of choice.

YIELD: 4 servings

Potato Peanut Soup

▶ **NUT**: PEANUT ▶ OIL-FREE POTENTIAL ▶ SOY-FREE POTENTIAL
▶ GLUTEN-FREE POTENTIAL

Even though it takes longer than 30 minutes to make, this one-pot soup is super easy, hearty, and healthy.

½ gallon (8 cups, or 1.9 L) vegetable broth

2 pounds (908 g) red, purple, or gold potatoes, cubed (leave the skin on)

1 cup (108 g) chopped or shredded carrots

1 white onion, roughly chopped

½ cup (50 g) chopped celery

4 cloves garlic, halved

1 cup (256 g) peanut butter

Cilantro Crema (page 110), for garnish

Dry-roasted peanuts, for garnish

Fresh basil, for garnish

Salt and pepper

Add the vegetable broth, potatoes, carrots, celery, and garlic to a large soup pot. Bring to a boil, reduce to a simmer, and simmer for 45 minutes. Stir in the peanut butter. Remove from the heat. Using an immersion blender, purée the soup until smooth. Ladle into bowls and drizzle liberally with Cilantro Crema. Top with fresh basil and dry-roasted peanuts. Add salt and pepper, to taste.

YIELD: 10 cups

Recipe Note

The color of your potatoes WILL affect the color of your soup.

Smoky Peas-tachio Soup
with Cashew Carrot Cream

▶ **NUTS**: PISTACHIO AND CASHEW ▶ SOY-FREE POTENTIAL ▶ GLUTEN-FREE POTENTIAL

Unlike thick, hearty, split pea soup, this soup uses frozen peas and is lighter and nuttier. (That could because it has nuts in it.)

FOR THE PEAS-TACHIO SOUP:

6 cups (1.4 L) vegetable broth

24 ounces (680 g) frozen peas

1 cup (124 g) dry-roasted pistachios

1 red onion, roughly chopped

5 cloves garlic, halved

½ teaspoon liquid smoke

FOR THE CASHEW CARROT CREAM:

1 cup (108 g) chopped carrots

½ cup (80 g) cashews, soaked at least 4 hours or simmered 15 to 20 minutes, rinsed and drained

½ cup (120 ml) unsweetened nut milk

2 tablespoons (28 g) unrefined coconut oil

FOR GARNISH:

Pistachios (optional)

To make the soup: Add all the ingredients, except the liquid smoke, to a large soup pot and bring to a boil. Reduce to a simmer, and cook for 30 minutes. After 30 minutes, stir in the liquid smoke. Using an immersion blender, or carefully transferring to a tabletop blender, purée until the desired texture is achieved. (I prefer mine a little chunky!)

To make the Cashew Carrot Cream: Steam the carrots until soft and tender. Add the steamed carrots, cashews, milk, and coconut oil to a blender, and purée until silky smooth.

Ladle the soup into serving bowls and garnish with a liberal drizzle of the cashew cream. For extra pizzazz, sprinkle a few pistachios on top.

YIELD: 4 meal-size servings (or 6 to 8 side-dish servings)

Autumnal Chestnut and Carrot Bisque

▶ **NUT**: CHESTNUT ▶ GLUTEN-FREE POTENTIAL

Perfect for the colder months with its roasted veggies and chestnut theme, we love to lighten up the flavors of this hearty soup by adding some of the sassy brine from our carrot pickles (page 112).

9 medium carrots, trimmed and peeled, chopped in 3 widthwise, each piece quartered lengthwise (aim for similar size)

1 tablespoon (15 ml) grapeseed or olive oil

2 tablespoons (30 ml) fresh orange juice

1 tablespoon (18 g) shiro (white) miso

1 large shallot or 1 medium white onion, peeled and quartered

3 cloves garlic (peeled but left whole)

5 ounces (142 g) shelled roasted chestnuts

4 cups (940 ml) vegetable broth (mushroom broth is great here)

½ teaspoon ground cumin

½ teaspoon garam masala

Salt and pepper

Splash of fresh lemon juice, to taste

Brine from carrot pickles (page 112) or ground sumac

Fresh parsley, chopped

Preheat the oven to 400°F (200°C, or gas mark 6). Place the carrots and oil in a 9 x 13-inch (23 x 33 cm) baking pan. In a small bowl, whisk to thoroughly combine the juice and miso. Pour on top of the carrots. Add the shallot and garlic to the pan, and fold to thoroughly combine. Bake in 10-minute increments, stirring after each increment, until the carrots are fully tender, about 30 to 40 minutes total depending on the cut-size and freshness of the carrots. Add the chestnuts when 10 minutes of roasting time are left.

Once ready, transfer the roasted preparation, broth, cumin, garam masala, salt, and pepper to a large pot. Bring to a low boil. Lower the heat and simmer uncovered for 15 minutes, stirring occasionally. Add just a splash of lemon juice to brighten the flavor, to taste. Using an immersion blender, blend the soup until still slightly chunky (careful of spatters). If you find the soup too thick, you can add up to 1 cup (235 ml) extra vegetable broth. Serve with about 1 tablespoon (15 ml) of brine (to taste), or a generous pinch sumac, and parsley on each serving.

YIELD: 6 servings

Recipe Note

For a soup that's slightly less thick but chunkier, reserve 1 to 1½ cups (155 to 233 g) roasted carrots before adding the broth to the vegetables. You can chop them up and add them after blending.

Cream of Pumpkin and Corn with Cashews and Lime

▶ **NUT**: CASHEW ▶ GLUTEN-FREE POTENTIAL ▶ SOY-FREE POTENTIAL

Born out of the necessity to finish leftovers from a large amount of puréed pumpkin, we couldn't be happier with this creamy, fall-centric soup made sunnier and zestier with ginger and lime.

3 cups (480 g) frozen sweet white or yellow corn, divided

1½ teaspoons melted coconut oil, grapeseed oil, or olive oil

1 cup (240 g) diced onion (any color)

2 cloves garlic, minced

½ teaspoon ginger powder or 2 teaspoons (5 g) grated fresh ginger

1 teaspoon coarse kosher salt

White pepper

Juice of 1½ limes (extra for garnish, if desired)

1 cup (120 g) raw cashew pieces (see Recipe Note)

2¼ cups (550 g) puréed cooked plain pumpkin

5 cups (1.2 L) no- or low-sodium vegetable broth

Lime zest, for garnish

Flat-leaf parsley, for garnish

Minced green parts of scallion, for garnish

Cayenne pepper, for garnish (optional)

Preheat the oven to 425°F (220°C, or gas mark 7). Place 2 cups (320 g) corn in a 9 x 13-inch (23 x 33 cm) baking pan. Roast until lightly browned for 20 to 25 minutes, stirring once halfway through. Set aside.

Brown the onion in the oil in a large pot for about 8 minutes on medium-high heat. Add the garlic, ginger, salt, and pepper, cooking for about 30 seconds. Deglaze the pot with lime juice. Add the cashews, pumpkin, remaining 1 cup (160 g) corn, and broth. Bring to a boil, lower the heat and simmer uncovered 25 minutes. With an immersion blender, blend until smooth. Alternatively, carefully transfer the hot soup to a regular blender.

Garnish each serving with roasted corn, lime zest and juice, chopped parsley, scallion, and cayenne pepper.

YIELD: 6 to 8 servings

Recipe Note

We found the simmering was enough to soften the cashews before blending. If your blender isn't the most efficient, soak the cashews for about 4 hours before making the soup (see method on page 14) for the smoothest results. Drain and rinse them well, and follow the recipe instructions as noted.

Southwest Peanut Sweet Potatoes

▶ **NUT**: PEANUT ▶ GLUTEN-FREE POTENTIAL ▶ SOY-FREE POTENTIAL

Sure these spicy sweet potatoes taste great on their own or as a side. But they also make a lovely addition to a salad or bowl, or even in quesadillas and tacos. You can use your favorite taco seasoning in this recipe, or you can make your own. We have included a taco seasoning recipe here for your convenience.

2 pounds (908 g) peeled and cubed sweet potatoes

2 tablespoons (30 ml) mild flavored oil

2 tablespoons (16 g) taco seasoning (see Recipe Note)

½ cup (56 g) chopped peanuts

1 shallot, sliced into thin rings

1 tablespoon (10 g) minced garlic

Preheat the oven to 375°F (190°C, or gas mark 5). Have ready a rimmed baking sheet lined with parchment, foil, or a reusable baking mat.

Toss the potatoes with the olive oil and taco seasoning to coat, and arrange in a single layer on the lined baking sheet. Roast for 30 minutes. Remove from the oven and toss with the peanuts, shallots, and garlic. Place back into the oven for an additional 20 minutes, or until the potatoes are soft and tender and the shallots and peanuts are slightly browned.

YIELD: 4 to 6 servings

Recipe Note

Here is our favorite recipe for taco seasoning. It was originally published in *500 Vegan Recipes*.

1 tablespoon (8 g) garlic powder

1 tablespoon (8 g) onion powder

1 tablespoon (13 g) sugar

1 tablespoon (6 g) ground cumin

1 tablespoon (7 g) paprika

2 tablespoons (14 g) chili powder (we use HOT chili powder)

1½ teaspoons salt

Place all the ingredients in a small airtight container and shake vigorously. Two tablespoons of this mix roughly equals one packet of store-bought taco seasoning.

YIELD: almost ½ cup (60 g)

Roasted Cabbage with Almond Lime Sauce

▶ **NUT**: ALMOND ▶ GLUTEN-FREE POTENTIAL ▶ SOY-FREE POTENTIAL

Here's a super simple way to dress up cabbage, which is roasted here for a fancier outcome with crispy edges. We make it a healthy and fiber-packed meal by serving it on top of any cooked whole grain of choice.

FOR THE SAUCE:

¼ cup (64 g) roasted crunchy almond butter

2 tablespoons to ¼ cup (30 to 60 ml) water

2 tablespoons (30 ml) fresh lime juice

1 teaspoon agave nectar or other natural liquid sweetener

1 clove garlic, grated or pressed

Salt

FOR THE CABBAGE:

1 head red or green cabbage, cut into ¾ inch (1.9 cm) round slices (if easier, cut into equal-size small wedges)

Grapeseed or olive oil, for brushing

Salt

Cooked whole grain of choice

Fresh parsley or cilantro leaves

Thinly sliced scallion (white and green parts)

Dry-roasted unsalted almonds, coarsely chopped

Lime wedges or lime zest

To make the sauce: Use a blender or vigorously whisk to thoroughly combine the ingredients (only 2 tablespoons, or 30 ml, water at first, add as needed to thin out). Set aside.

To make the cabbage: Preheat the oven to 400°F (200°C, or gas mark 6). Line a large rimmed baking sheet with parchment paper or a silicone baking mat. Lightly brush the cabbage with oil, and sprinkle salt to taste on top. Bake for 30 to 40 minutes, until crisp tender and lightly browned around the edges. You can chop the cabbage once cool enough to handle, or serve it as is.

Serve on top of cooked grain, drizzle with the sauce, and top with herbs, scallion, almonds, and lime wedges to squeeze, or zest to sprinkle on top.

YIELD: 4 servings, ¾ cup (180 ml) sauce

Roasted Hazelnut Brussels Sprouts

▶ **NUT**: HAZELNUT ▶ SOY-FREE ▶ GLUTEN-FREE POTENTIAL

This is an easy dish to prepare, and the maple plays nicely with the hazelnuts and mustard to give these sprouts a savory-sweet flavor that really works. This dish makes a good side dish. We like to add ours to a bowl of noochy noodles, or on top of salad greens and rice.

1 pound (454 g) fresh Brussels sprouts, cut in half

1 cup (135 g) raw hazelnuts without the shell

1 leek (about 4 ounces, or 114 g), cleaned and sliced into thin rounds, white and light green parts only

2 tablespoons (30 ml) olive oil

2 tablespoons (30 ml) pure maple syrup

1 teaspoon Dijon mustard

Salt and pepper

Preheat the oven to 375°F (190°C, or gas mark 5). Line a rimmed baking sheet with foil or parchment. Add the halved Brussels sprouts, hazelnuts, and leeks to a mixing bowl. In a separate small bowl, mix the together olive oil, maple syrup, and mustard. Add the mixture to the sprouts and toss to coat.

Spread in a single layer on the lined baking sheet. Sprinkle on salt and pepper to taste. Roast for 20 minutes. Remove from the oven, toss, and return to the oven for 10 more minutes, or until tender and the sprouts are browning around the edges. Serve immediately.

YIELD: 4 servings

Nut Butter Roasted Cauliflower

▶ **NUT**: PEANUT, CASHEW, OR ALMOND ▶ GLUTEN-FREE POTENTIAL ▶ OIL-FREE

We clearly have a soft spot for all combinations of roasted cruciferous vegetables and nut butters. Our favorite way to serve this oil-free, flavor-packed recipe is as a side dish to any basic whole grain of choice.

¼ cup (64 g) natural creamy or crunchy roasted peanut, cashew, or almond butter

¼ cup (60 ml) fresh orange juice

2 tablespoons (30 ml) tamari

1 tablespoon (15 ml) fresh lime juice

1 tablespoon (15 ml) brown rice vinegar

1 tablespoon (20 g) brown rice syrup, agave nectar, or pure maple syrup (optional)

1 clove garlic, grated or pressed

½ teaspoon red pepper flakes, to taste

½ teaspoon ginger powder or 2 teaspoons (4 g) grated fresh ginger

1 medium cauliflower head, trimmed and separated into florets

Dry-roasted peanuts, cashews, or almonds, for garnish

Chopped fresh cilantro or parsley, for garnish

Thinly sliced scallion, for garnish

In a large bowl, whisk to combine the peanut butter, orange juice, tamari, lime juice, vinegar, syrup, garlic, pepper flakes, and ginger. Add the florets, and fold to thoroughly combine. Place the florets in a 9 x 13-inch (23 x 33 cm) baking pan. Cover with a lid or foil, and marinate for a few hours in the refrigerator: morning until lunch is a good marinating time. Or lunch until dinner.

Retrieve the pan from the refrigerator and let stand at room temperature. Preheat the oven to 400°F (200°C, or gas mark 6). Remove the lid or foil (don't discard it), and bake for 10 minutes.

Stir and bake uncovered for another 5 to 10 minutes, or until tender (but not mushy) and still a little saucy (but not soupy). If the cauliflower is still too crunchy for your taste but the sauce is beginning to evaporate too much, cover with foil and cook until tender.

Let stand 10 minutes before serving, or serve at room temperature. Top with a handful of nuts, herbs, and scallion.

YIELD: 4 side-dish servings

Spicy Roasted Tahini Broccoli with Almonds

▶ **NUT AND SEED**: ALMOND AND SESAME ▶ GLUTEN-FREE POTENTIAL
▶ SOY-FREE POTENTIAL ▶ OIL-FREE POTENTIAL

This simple-to-prepare dish works as a side, in a bowl with rice and your favorite sauce, or even as a filling for tacos!

⅓ cup (85 g) tahini paste

¼ cup (60 ml) olive oil
or vegetable broth

3 tablespoons (45 ml) water

1 tablespoon (10 g) minced garlic

1 pound (454 g) broccoli florets

⅓ cup (30 g) sliced almonds

1 tablespoon (8 g) black or white
(or both!) sesame seeds

Red chili flakes, to taste

Salt and pepper

Preheat the oven to 350°F (180°C, or gas mark 4). Have ready a rimmed baking sheet lined with parchment, foil, or a reusable baking mat. In a medium bowl big enough for a pound of broccoli, add the tahini, olive oil, water, and garlic. Mix well to combine. Add in the broccoli and toss to coat thoroughly.

Place the broccoli in a single layer on the baking sheet and bake for 15 minutes. Remove from the oven and sprinkle on the sliced almonds, sesame seeds, and chili flakes. Return to the oven for an additional 15 minutes. Remove from the oven. Add salt and pepper to taste, and serve.

YIELD: 4 servings

Sweet Potato "Tartines" with Sriracha Peanut Butter

▶ **NUT**: PEANUT ▶ GLUTEN-FREE POTENTIAL ▶ SOY-FREE POTENTIAL

Ready for a gluten-free, deliciously salty, and super-simple appetizer or side dish? We spruced up beloved baked sweet potatoes with a ready-in-seconds peanut butter and sriracha spread that we can't get enough of.

We've kept the yield small—we can't control ourselves around these—but feel free to double, triple, or quadruple the recipe depending on what you need.

Peanut, coconut, or olive oil, for light brushing

2 medium sweet potatoes, brushed clean and sliced in half lengthwise

Coarse kosher salt

¼ cup (64 g) natural crunchy peanut butter

1 to 2 teaspoons (5 to 10 ml) sriracha sauce

1 to 2 teaspoons (5 to 10 ml) fresh lime juice, to taste

1½ tablespoons (15 g) minced red onion

¼ cup (4 g) fresh cilantro leaves

Chopped dry-roasted peanuts, to taste (optional)

Lime wedges, for garnish

Preheat the oven to 400°F (200°C, or gas mark 6). Have a small, rimmed baking sheet handy. Lightly brush the potatoes with oil, and sprinkle each flat side with a tiny pinch of salt. Place the potato halves face-side down on the baking sheet. Bake until tender (check with the point of a knife), about 25 to 30 minutes. The baking time will depend on the size and freshness of the potatoes, so check occasionally.

In the meantime, stir to combine the peanut butter, sriracha, and juice in a small bowl. Stir in the onion. If your peanut butter thickens a bit after the addition of the sriracha and juice, don't fret: the heat of the potatoes will help take it back to being perfectly spreadable.

When the potatoes are ready, apply approximately 1 tablespoon (16 g) of the sriracha butter on the surface of each potato half. Place the cilantro leaves on top and chopped peanuts, if desired. Serve immediately with lime wedges.

YIELD: 2 side-dish or 4 appetizer servings

Wilted Garlicky Greens with Nuts

▶ **NUTS AND SEEDS**: ALMOND, WALNUT, PINE NUT, AND SESAME
▶ SOY-FREE POTENTIAL ▶ GLUTEN-FREE POTENTIAL ▶ QUICK AND EASY

This quick preparation for bitter greens (kale, chard, arugula, collard . . .) is super easy. The end result is full of flavor that tastes great fresh out of the pan, as well as cold right out of the fridge.

1 to 3 tablespoons (15 to 45 ml) refined coconut or other mild flavored vegetable oil

¼ cup (23 g) sliced almonds

¼ cup (30 g) pine nuts

¼ cup (30 g) chopped walnuts

4 cloves thinly sliced garlic

8 ounces (227 g) bitter greens of choice, cut or torn into bite-size pieces

1 tablespoon (8 g) sesame seeds

Salt and pepper

Heat the oil over medium heat. Add the almonds, pine nuts, walnuts, and garlic to the pan, and sauté until fragrant and golden, about 3 minutes. Depending on how hearty your greens are, the cooking times will vary. Delicate greens can be cooked by removing the pan from the heat and adding in the greens to toss to cook and wilt. Heartier greens, like kale, may need a little time on the heat to fully cook. Stir in the sesame seeds. Season to taste with salt and pepper.

YIELD: 4 servings

Recipe Note

Golden raisins, currants, dried cranberries, or dried apricots make a great addition to this dish! Simply throw a handful into the pan at the same time as the nuts and garlic.

Pistachio Pesto Rice and Beans

▶ **NUT**: PISTACHIO ▶ SOY-FREE POTENTIAL ▶ GLUTEN-FREE POTENTIAL

There's more than one way to enjoy the quintessential vegan dish known as rice and beans! This recipe makes more pesto than is needed, but it freezes well. Pesto tastes great on all sorts of dishes, so don't fret, you'll figure out a way to use it up. Note that you can replace some, or all, of the oil with vegetable broth to make this pesto.

FOR THE PISTACHIO PESTO:

2 cups (60 g) baby spinach leaves

1 cup (124 g) dry-roasted pistachios

20 leaves fresh basil

1 cup (235 ml) olive oil

2 tablespoons (20 g) minced garlic

2 tablespoons (30 ml) fresh lemon juice

2 tablespoons (15 g) nutritional yeast

¼ teaspoon black pepper

Salt

FOR THE RICE AND BEANS:

1 cup (184 g) long-grain brown rice

2 cups (470 ml) water

1 can (15 ounces, or 425 g) white beans, drained and rinsed

2 cups (60 g) baby spinach

½ cup (62 g) dry-roasted pistachios

To make the pesto: Add all the ingredients to a blender and purée until smooth. Store in an airtight container in the refrigerator until ready to use.

To make the rice and beans: Add the rice and water to a rice cooker and follow the directions on your machine. If you do not have a rice cooker, bring water to a boil in medium saucepan. Stir in the rice. Return to a boil, reduce to a simmer, cover, and cook until the rice is tender and has absorbed all the liquid, 35 to 45 minutes. Once the rice is cooked, remove from the heat and fluff with a fork.

Transfer the rice to a mixing bowl; add the remaining ingredients and ½ cup (114 g) of the pesto. Toss to combine. This dish tastes great hot or cold, so serve as desired.

YIELD: 6 servings of rice and beans and 1½ cups (12 ounces, or 340 g) pesto

Recipe Note

Don't forget to save the aquafaba (the soaking liquid from the can of beans) for future recipes (pages 156 and 166)!

Mac(adamia) and Cheese

▶ **NUT**: MACADAMIA ▶ SOY-FREE POTENTIAL

Despite the seemingly sweet ingredients, this spin on mac and cheese is satisfyingly savory! Peas, broccoli, spinach, and crumbled tofu all make nice additions to this dish.

FOR THE MAC(ADAMIA) AND CHEESE:

1 cup (134 g) macadamia nuts, soaked at least 2 hours

1 cup (108 g) chopped carrots, steamed until soft

2½ cups (590 ml) full-fat coconut milk

¼ cup (30 g) nutritional yeast

1 tablespoon (10 g) minced garlic

¼ teaspoon dried thyme

¼ teaspoon ground coriander

¼ teaspoon ground turmeric

¼ teaspoon ground cumin

¼ teaspoon paprika

¼ teaspoon salt

¼ teaspoon black pepper

1 pound (454 g) short pasta of choice, prepared according to package instructions

FOR THE CRISPY PANKO TOPPING:

½ cup (40 g) panko bread crumbs

2 tablespoons (30 ml) melted coconut oil

¼ teaspoon paprika

¼ teaspoon dried parsley

¼ teaspoon onion powder

¼ teaspoon black pepper

To make the Mac(adamia) and Cheese: Add all of the ingredients, except the pasta, to a blender and purée until smooth. Add the mixture to the pasta and toss to coat. Place in a casserole dish. Preheat the oven to 375°F (190°C, or gas mark 5).

To make the Crispy Panko Topping: Mix together all of the ingredients and spread evenly all over Mac(adamia) and Cheese. Bake for 30 minutes, or until the topping is golden brown and crispy.

YIELD: 4 main-size or 8 side-dish servings

Sesame Pepper Pasta Salad

▶ **SEED**: SESAME ▶ GLUTEN-FREE POTENTIAL ▶ QUICK AND EASY

Readying the bell peppers and scallion takes no time if you carefully use a mandoline slicer. So this untraditional and sesame-loaded pasta salad can land on the potluck or dinner table rather quickly.

12 ounces (340 g) dry brown rice or whole wheat pasta

2 tablespoons (30 ml) toasted sesame oil

2 tablespoons (30 ml) brown rice vinegar

1 tablespoon (16 g) tahini paste

1 tablespoon (18 g) shiro (white) miso

1 tablespoon (15 ml) fresh lemon juice

1 teaspoon sambal oelek or sriracha sauce

1 to 2 cloves garlic, grated or pressed, to taste

2 red bell peppers, trimmed and cored, thinly sliced

1 tablespoon (8 g) toasted black or ivory sesame seeds, plus extra for garnish

Ume plum vinegar, to taste

Thinly sliced scallion (optional)

Cook the pasta to al dente according to the directions on the package (see Recipe Note), and quickly rinse under cold water. Drain well, and set aside.

In a large bowl, whisk to combine the oil, vinegar, tahini, miso, lemon juice, sambal oelek, and garlic. Add the pasta, bell peppers, and sesame seeds, and gently stir to combine with a rubber spatula. Let stand covered for 1 hour in the refrigerator. Serve with a dash of ume plum vinegar. (Don't be too generous, it is quite pungent and salty.) Garnish with a small handful of scallion and extra sesame seeds, if desired. Leftovers can be stored in an airtight container in the refrigerator for up 3 days.

YIELD: 4 to 6 servings

Recipe Note

Some brands of gluten-free brown rice pasta can have an unpleasant texture after refrigeration. If you know your go-to doesn't have this problem, use it here to keep the Asian theme going. If you're new to gluten-free pasta, we recommend checking out the instructions for proper cooking on glutenfreeonashoestring.com. If you aren't gluten-sensitive, whole wheat pasta will do just fine.

Tu-Nut Salad

▶ **NUTS AND SEEDS**: PECAN, CASHEW, ALMOND, AND SUNFLOWER SEED
▶ GLUTEN-FREE POTENTIAL ▶ SOY-FREE POTENTIAL

This nutty salad gets its seafood-y flavor from wakame seaweed which becomes soft and tender when cooked. Make sure to get "cut" wakame, or your pieces will be huge once boiled. You can use this salad on a sandwich, in a wrap, on top of mixed greens, on crackers, as a dip with tortilla chips . . . .

FOR THE SALAD:

1 quart (4 cups, or 45 ml) water

¼ cup (16 g) dried and cut wakame seaweed

2 tablespoons (20 g) minced garlic

1 teaspoon salt

1 cup (99 g) pecans, roughly chopped

½ cup (56 g) cashews, roughly chopped

½ cup (64 g) sunflower kernels

½ cup (45 g) sliced or (54 g) slivered almonds

¼ cup (32 g) pepitas

1 cup (101 g) chopped celery

½ cup (80 g) diced red onion

½ cup (70 g) diced red bell pepper

½ cup (30 g) chopped fresh parsley

½ cup (50 g) chopped scallion

3 tablespoons (45 g) pickle relish or cucumber

FOR THE DRESSING:

1 cup (224 g) Simple Cashew Mayo (page 27) or any store-bought vegan mayo (use a soy-free variety for a soy-free dish)

1 tablespoon (15 ml) apple cider vinegar

1 teaspoon Dijon mustard

1 teaspoon dried dill, or 1 tablespoon (4 g) fresh chopped dill

½ teaspoon black salt (kala namak)

½ teaspoon onion powder

¼ teaspoon paprika

To make the salad: Add the water, seaweed, garlic, and salt to a pot, and bring to a boil. Add in the pecans, cashews, sunflower kernels, almonds, and pepitas. Return to a boil, reduce to a simmer, cover and simmer for 20 minutes, returning to stir occasionally. Remove from the heat. Drain the liquid through a fine-mesh strainer and cool completely.

To make the dressing: While it's cooling, make the dressing by whisking all the ingredients together. Refrigerate until ready to use.

Once cooled, mix in the celery, onion, bell pepper, parsley, scallion, relish, and dressing. Keep in an airtight container in the refrigerator for up to 1 week.

YIELD: 8 to 10 servings

Sunflower Almond Buffalo Coleslaw

▶ **NUT AND SEED**: ALMOND AND SUNFLOWER SEED ▶ QUICK AND EASY
▶ SOY-FREE POTENTIAL

This coleslaw is great for potlucks, parties, and tastes amazing on a sandwich with fried zucchinis or BBQ jackfruit. It's got just a touch of heat that pairs lovely with the cool crunch of the cabbage and the chew of the cherries.

1 small head (about 4 cups, or 280 g) finely shredded green cabbage

1 cup (235 ml) Creamy Sunflower Buffalo Sauce (page 29)

½ cup (64 g) sunflower kernels

½ cup (45 g) sliced or (54 g) slivered almonds

½ cup (64 g) dried cherries (or raisins, currants, or cranberries)

½ cup (8 g) chopped fresh cilantro

½ cup (50 g) chopped celery

1 teaspoon dried dill, or 1 tablespoon (4 g) fresh dill

½ teaspoon black pepper

¼ teaspoon red chili flakes

Add all the ingredients to a large mixing bowl and toss until well combined. Store in an airtight container in the refrigerator until ready to serve. This one tastes even better the next day!

YIELD: 8 servings

Solid Potato Salad

▶ **NUT AND SEED:** CASHEW AND PEPITA ▶ GLUTEN-FREE POTENTIAL
▶ SOY-FREE POTENTIAL ▶ OIL-FREE POTENTIAL

We came across a video of the Ross Sisters doing some amazing acrobatics while singing about solid potato salad back in 1944. But what is a solid potato salad? We think it has two meanings. 1. Potato salad that is really, really good, like the Ross Sisters say, "That's solid, Jack!", and 2. A potato salad that is made with whole or cut potatoes, not smashed or mashed potatoes. Note that this recipe, as written, makes a really dressed salad. If you prefer yours less dressed, you can cut the dressing amount down or up the amount of potatoes to your liking.

FOR THE SALAD:

2 pounds (908 g) potatoes of choice (we like fingerlings or baby reds) cubed

1 cup (160 g) diced red onion

1 cup (101 g) chopped celery

1 cup (134 g) green peas

½ cup (50 g) chopped scallion

½ cup (32 g) pepitas, raw or toasted (your choice!)

¼ cup (24 g) vegan bacon bits (optional)

Salt and pepper

FOR THE DRESSING:

2 cups (168 g) cashews, soaked overnight, or boiled for 20 minutes, rinsed and drained

1 cup (235 ml) vegetable broth

¼ cup plus 1 tablespoon (75 ml) mild-flavored oil, or additional vegetable broth

3 tablespoons (45 ml) white vinegar

1 tablespoon (15 ml) fresh lemon juice

1 tablespoon (15 g) Dijon mustard

2 teaspoons (6 g) garlic powder

1 teaspoon prepared yellow mustard

½ teaspoon paprika

¼ teaspoon ground turmeric

½ teaspoon black salt (kala namak)

1 teaspoon dried parsley

1 teaspoon dried dill

Add the potatoes to a pot of water and bring to a boil. Boil until fork tender but still, well, solid. While the potatoes are boiling, make the dressing.

To make the dressing: Add all of the ingredients, except the parsley and dill, to a blender. Purée until smooth. Stir in the parsley and dill. Drain the potatoes and rinse under cold water to cool.

To make the salad: Return the potatoes to the pot. Add the dressing and remaining salad ingredients, except bacon bits, to the potatoes and toss to mix. Season to taste with salt and pepper. Top with the bacon bits just before serving.

YIELD: 8 servings

Recipe Note

You can boil your cashews and then make the dressing right in the pot using an immersion blender.

Cauliflower Pecan Tabouli

▶ **NUT**: PECAN ▶ GLUTEN-FREE POTENTIAL ▶ SOY-FREE POTENTIAL ▶ QUICK AND EASY

No cooking required! If you've got mad knife skills, feel free to get chopping. If not, use those power tools. A food processor will make quick work of this super-simple grain-free salad.

1 head (about 7 cups, 30 ounces, or 851 g) cauliflower, finely chopped

2 cups (198 g) pecans, finely chopped

1 bunch parsley, finely chopped

½ cup (120 ml) olive oil

1 medium yellow onion, finely chopped

3 tablespoons (30 g) minced garlic

2 tablespoons (30 ml) fresh lemon juice

Salt and pepper

Mix it all the ingredients up in a large mixing bowl and refrigerate until ready to serve. This salad is very hearty and can be made ahead of time. In fact, it tastes even better the next day, after the flavors really meld together.

YIELD: 8 servings

Recipe Note

Chopped tomatoes also make a nice addition to this salad, and they take the flavor profile up a notch. You can also replace 2 tablespoons (30 ml) of the olive oil with sesame oil for extra oomph.

Sweet Potato Salad
with Tahini Sumac Dressing

▶ **SEED:** SESAME ▶ GLUTEN-FREE POTENTIAL ▶ SOY-FREE POTENTIAL

In order to make the oven roasting time worthwhile, we've made the potato yield 4 times as large as what's needed for the small salad yield. The salad portion, on the other hand, makes for a big and bold lunch salad that can serve one person with a good appetite, or two as a side dish. That way you can just reheat the potato left-overs and have fresh salad for the next few days. If you find the dressing a bit too thick to coat the salad easily, follow the instructions on page 28 to thin it out.

FOR THE POTATOES:

4 small (1 pound, or 454 g) sweet potatoes, cut into small bites

1 tablespoon (15 ml) grapeseed oil

1 tablespoon (15 ml) fresh lime juice

1 teaspoon coarse kosher salt

Generous ½ teaspoon ground cumin

Generous ½ teaspoon smoked paprika

½ teaspoon onion powder

Nonstick cooking spray or oil spray

FOR THE SALAD:

1 generous cup (80 g) finely shredded green cabbage

1 small avocado, pitted, peeled, and chopped

4 large red radishes, thinly sliced

2 to 4 tablespoons (10 to 20 g) thinly sliced scallion (white and green parts), to taste

2 tablespoons (30 ml) Tahini Sumac Dressing (page 28), to taste (thin out if needed)

Chopped fresh parsley or chives

Toasted sesame seeds

To make the potatoes: Preheat the oven to 425°F (220°C, or gas mark 7). Combine all the ingredients in a large bowl. Lightly coat a 9 x 13-inch (23 x 33 cm) baking pan with cooking spray. Transfer the potatoes to the pan. Roast until just tender and browned, about 25 minutes. Be sure to stir frequently, at least every 10 minutes, to prevent burning.

To assemble the salad: Place the cabbage, avocado, radishes, scallion, one-quarter of the warm potatoes, and the dressing in a large bowl. Fold to thoroughly combine. Transfer to a plate, top with herbs and seeds, and dig in.

Store the cooled potato leftovers in an airtight container in the refrigerator for up to 3 days, and slowly reheat in a dry, medium-hot pan until slightly crispy.

YIELD: 1 to 2 servings

Pistachio Plateful of Produce with Pomegranate Vinaigrette

▸ **NUT**: PISTACHIO ▸ GLUTEN-FREE POTENTIAL ▸ QUICK AND EASY ▸ SOY-FREE POTENTIAL

We know that traveling vegans can have an aversion to salads because they are often an unavoidable go-to at vegan-unfriendly restaurants. But there's salad, and then there's *salad*. Avocado, chickpeas, pomegranate molasses, and pistachios, to name but a few of the ingredients—this *salad* clearly is no mere salad. You must try the dressing on steamed or roasted vegetables, too.

1 tablespoon (15 ml) roasted pistachio oil or grapeseed oil

2 tablespoons (30 ml) pomegranate molasses (page 17)

1 tablespoon (15 ml) white balsamic vinegar

½ teaspoon mild Dijon mustard

1 clove garlic, grated or pressed

Generous pinch coarse kosher salt

Generous pinch ground sumac

Freshly ground pepper

2 Persian cucumbers, thinly sliced

2 small heirloom tomatoes (yellow is pretty here), thinly sliced

2 large or 4 small red radishes, thinly sliced

½ cup (85 g) cooked chickpeas

⅓ cup (40 g) roasted pistachios, chopped

1 avocado, pitted, peeled, and sliced

2 generous handfuls microgreens, thoroughly washed and dried

1 scallion, thinly sliced

Chopped fresh parsley or cilantro or a combination, to taste

In a small bowl, whisk to thoroughly combine the oil, pomegranate molasses, vinegar, mustard, garlic, salt, sumac, and pepper. Set aside.

Decorate 2 large plates each with 1 sliced cucumber, 1 sliced tomato, 1 or 2 sliced radishes, ¼ cup (41 g) chickpeas, 2½ tablespoons (20 g) pistachios, half of the avocado slices, 1 handful microgreens, half of the scallion, and the chopped herbs.

Whisk the dressing again to emulsify, then drizzle on top of each plate. There will be enough dressing for both plates. Serve immediately.

YIELD: 2 servings

Pecan Radicchio and Grilled Apple Salad

▶ **NUT**: PECAN ▶ GLUTEN-FREE POTENTIAL ▶ SOY-FREE POTENTIAL

Word to the wise: consider doubling the amount of pecans here. You might find yourself sampling the batch while you're busy fixing the rest of the salad. The good news is that the pecan portion is a breeze to prepare—with a super short ingredient list that doesn't skimp on flavor.

FOR THE PECANS:

¾ cup (90 g) raw pecan pieces

1 teaspoon agave nectar or pure maple syrup

1 teaspoon grapeseed or olive oil

Couple pinches coarse kosher salt

1 teaspoon minced fresh rosemary

FOR THE APPLES:

1 large tart apple or 2 small, quartered and cored, each quarter quartered

2 tablespoons (30 ml) unsweetened, unfiltered apple cider (not hard cider) or apple juice

FOR THE DRESSING:

2 tablespoons (30 ml) unsweetened, unfiltered apple cider (not hard cider) or apple juice

2 tablespoons (30 ml) toasted walnut oil, grapeseed or olive oil

1 tablespoon (15 g) mild Dijon mustard

2 teaspoons (10 ml) apple cider vinegar

½ teaspoon coarse kosher salt

1 clove garlic, grated or pressed

Ground pepper

1 tablespoon (20 g) agave nectar or pure maple syrup, to taste (optional)

FOR THE SALAD:

6 packed cups (300 g) chopped radicchio

Fresh curly parsley, chopped

To make the pecans: Preheat the oven to 300°F (150°C, or gas mark 2). Combine all the ingredients in a small bowl. Place on a small, rimmed baking sheet lined with parchment paper, and bake for 6 minutes. Stir, and bake for another 6 minutes, or until the nuts are fragrant and dry. Be careful not to let burn. Let cool completely.

To make the dressing: Whisk to emulsify all of the ingredients in a small bowl. Add the sweetener at the end, if desired. Refrigerate until ready to use, and whisk again before use.

To make the apples: Toss the apple slices together with the cider in a large bowl. Heat a grill or grill pan, and sear the slices until grill marks appear, 2 to 3 minutes on each side. Don't let the apple slices go mushy. Set aside, and chop once cooled.

To assemble the salad: Place the radicchio, parsley, and apples in a large bowl. Add dressing to taste, and top each serving with a handful of pecans. Serve immediately.

YIELD: 3 to 4 servings, ⅓ cup (80 ml) dressing

Recipe Note

Not a fan of radicchio? Try arugula or a mix of your favorite greens.

6

ENDING THINGS ON A SWEET NUT

See Nuts Get Their Just Desserts

We come bearing sweet gifts: from wiser choices to utter decadence, nuts and seeds come through for us all once again in this closing chapter. Whether you're more of a fruit lover or want to go all out with, say, the royal pairing of peanut butter and chocolate, get ready to meet your new favorite dessert ever!

Pineapple Nut Curry Clusters

▶ **NUTS AND SEEDS**: CASHEW, PEANUT, AND SESAME ▶ GLUTEN-FREE POTENTIAL
▶ OIL-FREE POTENTIAL

These nuts are sweet, but they have a savory undertone with a touch of spice that makes them addictive! Try them broken up over ice cream or yogurt.

1 cup (220 g) tightly packed brown sugar

2 tablespoons (30 ml) agave nectar or other liquid sweetener

2 tablespoons (30 ml) mirin

1 tablespoon (15 ml) tamari

2 teaspoons (4 g) yellow curry powder

⅛ teaspoon cayenne pepper, to taste (optional)

1 cup (112 g) cashews

1 cup (112 g) peanuts

1 cup (5 ounces, or g) chopped dried pineapple

2 tablespoons (16 g) sesame seeds, black or white

Have ready a rimmed baking sheet lined with waxed paper or parchment.

Add the brown sugar, agave, mirin, tamari, curry powder, and cayenne pepper to a pot. Heat over medium heat until the sugar is melted and dissolved and begins to bubble. Stir often. You want to make sure the sugar is completely dissolved, but you do not want to burn the sugar. This should take 5 to 7 minutes.

Add in the remaining ingredients and stir to mix. Pour onto the lined baking sheet and spread evenly into a single layer. Allow to cool completely and break into bite-size pieces. Store in an airtight container.

YIELD: 1½ pounds (12 ounces, or 340 g)

Baked Pears

▶ **NUT**: PECAN ▶ GLUTEN-FREE POTENTIAL ▶ OIL-FREE ▶ SOY-FREE POTENTIAL

Celine grew up eating the delicious baked apples her mom used to make. This alternate version made with pears—free of refined sugars and as natural as can be—boasts a generous amount of crunchy, buttery pecans, and loads of flavor.

2 large D'Anjou (or other) pears, halved and cored

Generous ½ cup (70 g) raw pecan pieces, chopped

4 Medjool dates, pitted and chopped

Generous ½ teaspoon pure vanilla extract

Generous ½ teaspoon ground cinnamon

¼ cup (60 ml) unfiltered, unsweetened apple cider (not hard cider) or apple juice, plus extra for basting

Vegan vanilla ice cream or yogurt, for garnish (optional)

Preheat the oven to 350°F (180°C, or gas mark 4). Have a 9-inch (23 cm) square baking dish handy. Fit the pear halves in it.

In a medium bowl, stir to combine the pecans, dates, vanilla, cinnamon, and ¼ cup (60 ml) cider. Set aside for a couple of minutes to moisten. Fit the mixture into the cored pear halves, pressing down gently to pile it in. Add a couple of extra teaspoons (10 ml) of cider on each pear to baste.

Bake for 25 to 30 minutes, until the pears are tender, and the filling is caramelized and golden brown. Make sure to baste the pears and their filling every 10 minutes. Use a teaspoon to scoop the apple cider that lands at the bottom of the dish, or add extra teaspoons as needed if there isn't much at the bottom of the dish. If the pears aren't tender yet but the filling is browning up too quickly, use a piece of foil to loosely cover the tops and continue baking. Let stand 5 to 10 minutes before serving as is, or with a scoop of vegan vanilla ice cream or yogurt.

YIELD: 4 servings

Recipe Notes

• You can add a pinch ground cloves, ginger, allspice, and nutmeg at the same time as the cinnamon if you'd like.

• If you cannot find pretty, large pears, use 4 smaller ones instead. As long as the filling fits nicely without being skimpy or falling out, you're good to go. Note that using smaller pears, as well as ripeness levels, will alter the baking time. So keep an eye on the pears as they bake and follow the doneness cues.

Brigadei-raw

▶ **NUT**: BRAZIL NUT ▶ GLUTEN-FREE POTENTIAL ▶ OIL-FREE ▶ QUICK AND EASY
▶ SOY-FREE POTENTIAL

Brigadeiro translates to "brigadier" from Portuguese. It is the name of a Brazilian chocolate-caramel bonbon made of cocoa powder, condensed milk, and butter. Our raw version is quite a bit less decadent (but no less delicious), made instead with Brazil nuts and refined coconut oil for richness, and dates for a caramel-like flavor.

¼ cup (42 g) raw Brazil nuts

2 tablespoons (18 g) cacao nibs

10 pitted Medjool or other favorite dates

1 teaspoon brown rice syrup, date syrup, barley malt syrup, or pure maple syrup

1 teaspoon partially melted coconut oil (like softened butter)

½ teaspoon pure vanilla extract

Pinch coarse kosher salt

Coating: Unsweetened cocoa powder, hulled hemp seeds, lightly toasted shredded coconut, or extra cacao nibs

Place the nuts and cacao nibs in a food processor, and blend until finely ground. Add the dates, syrup, oil, vanilla, and salt. Process until a rather smooth and compact paste forms. Set aside.

Grab 1½ teaspoons of the date paste, and shape into a round bonbon. Place on a plate lined with waxed paper. Repeat with remaining paste. You should get 20 bonbons in all, but this might vary slightly. Roll each bonbon into the coating of choice. The quantity will vary: at least 1 tablespoon (5 g) cocoa powder, 1 tablespoon (10 g) hemp seeds, or 1 tablespoon (4 g) shredded coconut; more for cacao nibs. Place the bonbons back on the plate. Store in an airtight container in the refrigerator for at least 1 hour, or until ready to eat. Leftovers can be kept in an airtight container in the refrigerator for up to 4 days.

YIELD: 20 bonbons

Pistachio Macarons with Orange Ganache Filling

▶ **NUTS**: ALMOND AND PISTACHIO ▶ GLUTEN-FREE POTENTIAL
▶ OIL-FREE POTENTIAL ▶ SOY-FREE POTENTIAL

French macarons are extremely labor intensive and painstakingly slow to make. The technique used here was developed by the extremely talented Charis who runs the blog Floral Frosting (floralfrosting.blogspot.com) and perfected the vegan French macaron. We highly recommend watching a YouTube video on the process known as *macaronage*, because words just do not do it justice. You may fail at your first try—or even your second or third try. Just remember you must be patient and consistent. With some practice you will be able to make amazing French macarons.

FOR THE SHELLS:

½ cup (120 ml) aquafaba (see notes on page 167)

½ cup (96 g) granulated raw sugar

1 teaspoon pure vanilla extract

1¼ cups (120 g) almond meal, finely ground into a powder

½ cup (62 g) pistachios, finely ground into a powder

½ cup (60 g) powdered sugar

¼ cup (31 g) pistachios, chopped

Zest from one orange

FOR THE FILLING:

½ cup (120 ml) almond milk

½ cup (44 g) vegan chocolate chips

2 teaspoons (10 ml) orange extract

To make the shells: Start by reducing your aquafaba to ⅓ cup (80 ml) by simmering it over medium heat for about 5 minutes. Cool to room temperature. Add the reduced aquafaba to the bowl of your stand mixer and whip using a whisk attachment until soft peaks form. Slowly incorporate the sugar, 1 tablespoon (12 g) at a time. Then incorporate the vanilla. Continue to whip until thick and glossy. Your goal is the consistency of marshmallow fluff.

In a separate bowl, mix together the almond meal, ground pistachios, and powdered sugar. Press through a sieve to remove any large lumps. Pour half the dry mixture into the aquafaba fluff. Use a spatula to fold the ingredients together, pressing the dry ingredients down into the meringue until everything is incorporated well. Add the remaining dry mixture and fold into the batter.

Use the *macaronage* technique to fully incorporate the batter. Press the batter against the side of the bowl with the spatula, then fold it over and swirl it in a figure eight pattern. Repeat this process about 20 times. Your batter should be glossy, but run off your spatula in ribbons that sink into the remaining batter within seconds. (Watch the video!)

Recipe Notes

- When making macarons, the weather can affect your final outcome tremendously. Hot, humid days are not best suited for macaron making. High humidity prevents the cookies from drying out completely and prevents the magical "feet" from forming. Footless macarons still taste delicious, they simply don't have feet.

- To make Peanut Butter Cup Macarons, replace the ground pistachios with peanut butter powder. Switch the orange extract in the ganache for vanilla. Sprinkle cocoa on top instead of chopped pistachios and leave off the orange zest.

Line two baking sheets with parchment paper. (Silicone mats are not recommended for this recipe.) Transfer your batter into a piping bag. Pipe 15 cookies onto each sheet, approximately 1½ inches (7 cm) in diameter. Pick up the cookie tray about 2 feet (60 cm) off the countertop and drop it. This will help get rid of air bubbles and aid in the forming of the "feet." Top 15 of the cookies with chopped pistachios and orange zest and set aside to rest for 2 to 3 hours.

Place in a cold oven. Close the oven and turn it to 235°F (113°C) and bake for 30 minutes. Turn off the oven, and let the shells rest inside the oven for an additional 30 minutes. Crack the oven door and let them sit another 15 minutes before finally removing them from the oven to cool for an additional 2 hours.

Make the filling: Bring the milk to a boil in a small saucepan. As soon as it begins to bubble, remove it from the heat and whisk in the chocolate chips until they are melted. Mix in the orange extract.

Once the cookies have completely cooled, spread a small amount of filling on the plain cookies. Sandwich the ganache with a cookie topped with pistachios. Store in a very dry place until ready to serve.

YIELD: 30 macarons

Banana Nut Cookies with Oats and Cranberries

▶ **NUT**: ALMOND AND PEANUT ▶ SOY-FREE POTENTIAL

Hearty enough for breakfast and just sweet enough for dessert. Our favorite time to enjoy these nutty-fruity cookies is . . . anytime.

2 cups (156 g) quick-cooking oats

1 cup (120 g) whole wheat pastry flour

1 cup (96 g) almond meal

1 teaspoon baking soda

1 teaspoon baking powder

½ teaspoon salt

1 cup (235 ml) almond milk

½ cup (110 g) packed brown sugar

½ cup (120 ml) pure maple syrup

¼ cup (64 g) peanut butter

¼ cup (60 ml) melted coconut oil

¼ cup (60 ml) aquafaba (the liquid from a can of chickpeas)

2 teaspoons (10 ml) pure vanilla extract

1 cup (100 g) crushed banana chips

1 cup (90 g) sliced almonds

1 cup (122 g) dried cranberries (or raisins)

½ cup (60 g) finely shredded coconut

Preheat the oven to 350°F (180°C, or gas mark 4). Have ready a baking sheet lined with parchment or a reusable baking mat.

Add the oats, flour, almond meal, baking soda, baking powder, and salt to a large mixing bowl. In a separate bowl, mix together the milk, sugar, brown sugar, maple syrup, peanut butter, coconut oil, aquafaba, and vanilla. Add wet to dry and mix until well combined. Fold in the banana chips, almonds, cranberries, and coconut.

Drop 2 heaping tablespoons (35 g) of dough onto the baking sheet and press slightly to flatten. Place 12 cookies on the sheet. Bake 10 to 12 minutes, or until golden. Remove from the oven and allow to cool for 5 minutes before transferring to a cooling rack.

YIELD: 36 cookies

Fruity Cashew Oat Squares

▶ **NUT AND SEED**: CASHEW AND CHIA ▶ OIL-FREE POTENTIAL ▶ SOY-FREE POTENTIAL

These cashew-packed squares are treat-like enough for dessert, but not too decadent for breakfast. Switch the nut or fruit according to the season. We used apricot jam and mango cubes for the picture, but you could match other jams and fruits too. Let your imagination run wild! If using a gluten-free flour blend, it can also have gluten-free potential.

FOR THE BASE AND FILLING:

Nonstick cooking spray, oil spray, or parchment paper

½ cup (160 g) all-fruit apricot jam

2 tablespoons (20 g) chia seeds

⅓ cup (106 g) pure maple syrup or agave nectar

⅓ cup (85 g) roasted cashew butter

1 teaspoon pure vanilla extract

¼ teaspoon coarse kosher salt

1 cup (120 g) whole wheat pastry flour

½ cup (60 g) cashew meal

3 large apricots, pitted and sliced or 1½ cups (240 g) small mango chunks

FOR THE TOPPING:

¾ cup (72 g) old-fashioned rolled oats

3 tablespoons (23 g) cashew meal

3 tablespoons (60 g) pure maple syrup or agave nectar

3 tablespoons (48 g) roasted cashew butter

1 teaspoon pure vanilla extract

½ teaspoon ground cinnamon

Pinch coarse kosher salt

To make the base and filling: Preheat the oven to 350°F (180°C, or gas mark 4). Lightly coat an 8-inch (20 cm) square baking pan with cooking spray, or line with parchment paper. In a small bowl, stir to combine the jam and chia seeds. Set aside. In a medium bowl, stir to combine the maple syrup, cashew butter, vanilla, and salt. Add the flour and meal on top. Stir or knead to thoroughly combine. Break into large crumbles, place in the prepared pan, and press down to cover the pan in an even layer. (Keep the bowl handy.)

Spread the jam mixture evenly on top, leaving less than ½ inch (1.27 cm) around the edges. Cover the mixture evenly with apricot slices; overlapping is fine.

To make the topping: Use the same bowl to combine all the ingredients. Evenly crumble the topping over the fruit, pressing down slightly.

Bake for 20 minutes, or until golden brown. If browning too quickly, loosely cover with a piece of foil. Turn off the oven, and leave the pan in the oven for another 15 minutes. Let cool completely before serving. Store the tightly covered leftovers in the refrigerator for up to 2 days.

YIELD: One 8-inch (20 cm) pan, about 9 servings

Coco-Hazelnut Fudge Brownies

▶ **NUT**: HAZELNUT

These brownies are fudgy and dense. They'll pair up well with a nice tall glass of your favorite nut milk.

1¾ cups (415 ml) full-fat coconut milk

1 cup (176 g) vegan semisweet chocolate chips

⅓ cup (80 ml) coconut oil

⅓ cup (113 g) applesauce

2 teaspoons (10 ml) pure vanilla extract

2 cups (240 g) whole wheat pastry flour or (250 g) all-purpose flour

1 cup (192 g) granulated raw sugar

½ cup (110 g) packed brown sugar

½ cup (40 g) unsweetened cocoa powder

½ teaspoon baking powder

¼ teaspoon baking soda

¼ teaspoon fine salt

1½ cups (173 g) chopped hazelnuts, divided

¼ teaspoon coarse salt

Preheat the oven to 350°F (180°C, or gas mark 4). Line a 9 x 13-inch (23 x 33 cm) baking dish with 2 pieces of parchment paper, one going in each direction, with plenty of overhang, so that you can easily lift the brownies out of the dish once they are cool.

In a small sauce pot, bring the milk to a boil. As soon as it begins to boil, add in the chocolate chips and stir until completely melted. Remove from the heat and stir in the oil, applesauce, and vanilla.

In a separate bowl, mix together the flour, sugar, brown sugar, cocoa, baking powder, baking soda, and fine salt. Mix wet ingredients into dry, and mix until well combined. Fold in 1 cup (115 g) of the hazelnuts. Pour the batter into the baking dish.

Sprinkle the remaining hazelnuts and coarse salt all over the top of the batter. Bake for 35 to 40 minutes, or until a toothpick inserted into the center comes out clean. Remove from the oven and allow to cool completely. These taste great chilled overnight. Once cool, cut into squares and enjoy.

YIELD: 16 brownies

Peanut Butter and Jelly Thumbprints

▶ **NUT**: PEANUT ▶ SOY-FREE POTENTIAL ▶ OIL-FREE POTENTIAL

Who would have thought such a simple list of ingredients could lead to such a fun cookie?

2 cups (240 g) whole wheat pastry flour or (250 g) all-purpose flour

½ teaspoon baking powder

½ teaspoon baking soda

2 cups (512 g) peanut butter

1¾ cups (420 g) of your favorite flavored jam or jelly, divided

Preheat the oven to 350°F (180°C, or gas mark 4). Have ready 2 or 3 baking sheets lined with parchment or a reusable baking mat.

In a mixing bowl, sift together the flour, baking powder, and baking soda. Add in the peanut butter and 1 cup (240 g) jelly. This recipe was made with creamy no-stir peanut butter. Because the moisture content of peanut butters can vary, you may need a little extra flour if yours is very wet. If it is very dry, you'll need less.

Mix well. Make sure all the ingredients are well incorporated. Using 2 tablespoons (30 g) of dough, roll into balls and then flatten slightly into a disk shape. Place on a prepared baking sheet.

Bake for 8 minutes. Remove from the oven and make a depression in each cookie, using your thumb or the back side of a tablespoon-size measuring spoon, as it has a nice round, deep well. Fill the depressions with 1 teaspoon of additional jelly or jam. Bake an additional 8 minutes. Let cool about 10 minutes before transferring to a wire rack to cool completely.

YIELD: 30 cookies

Rosewater Pistachio Meringues

▶ **NUT**: PISTACHIO ▶ SOY-FREE POTENTIAL ▶ OIL-FREE POTENTIAL
▶ GLUTEN-FREE POTENTIAL

Meringues are another classic dessert us vegans thought were out of reach because the main ingredient is egg whites. With the discovery of aquafaba (see notes on page 167), meringues are now within easy grasp! This recipe is courtesy of Erin Wysocarski of the incredible blog Olives for Dinner (olivesfordinner.com). She took the basic three-ingredient meringue recipe from Goose Wohlt (the mastermind who discovered aquafaba) and made it her own. Her recipe calls for a food dye made from red radish and hibiscus. That type of food dye can be difficult to find, and we opted to use ground, dried hibiscus flowers as the source of color. Hibiscus flowers are quite delicious, with a tart floral essence that works well with the rosewater and pistachios.

1 cup (235 ml) aquafaba

1 cup (192 g) granulated raw sugar (such as Zulka)

¼ cup (10 g) dried hibiscus flowers, ground into a fine powder

2 tablespoons (30 ml) rosewater (or 1 teaspoon rosewater extract)

1 teaspoon xanthan gum

½ cup (62 g) finely chopped pistachios

Add the aquafaba to the bowl of your stand mixer and whip on high speed using a whisk attachment until stiff peaks form. This can take up to 30 minutes. With the mixer still whipping, slowly incorporate the sugar, then the powdered hibiscus, then the rosewater, and finally the xanthan gum. Transfer the mixture into a piping bag fitted with your largest star tip, or a resealable plastic bag with the corner snipped off.

Preheat the oven to 235°F (115°C). Line 2 baking sheets with parchment. Reusable baking mats are not recommended. You can make these any size you like, but smaller sizes (silver dollars) seem to yield the best results, especially for beginner aquafaba-ers. Pipe the mixture onto the baking sheets in small mounds, leaving at least 1 inch (2.5 cm) between cookies. Sprinkle liberally with chopped pistachios.

Bake for 2 hours then turn off the oven and crack it open slightly. Leave the cookies in the oven overnight (8 hours!) to dry out completely. Note that meringues will absorb moisture right out of thin air. Make sure not to leave them out on the counter too long, and keep them stored in an airtight container in a dry place.

YIELD: About 30 silver dollar–size meringues

Pineapple Coconut Macadamia Freezer Pops

▶ **NUT**: MACADAMIA NUT ▶ SOY-FREE POTENTIAL ▶ GLUTEN-FREE POTENTIAL
▶ OIL-FREE POTENTIAL

This creamy tropical treat is super easy to make and, let's face it, freezer pops are super fun to eat!

1½ cups (355 ml) full-fat coconut milk

1 cup (235 ml) pineapple juice

½ cup (60 g) shredded coconut

½ cup (67 g) macadamia nuts, finely chopped

¼ cup (48 g) raw sugar

1 cup (181 g) pineapple bits, finely chopped

Add all the ingredients, except the chopped pineapple, to a pot. Stir and bring to a boil. Reduce to a simmer and simmer for 10 minutes, stirring regularly. Remove from the heat and stir in the pineapple bits. Cool completely. Carefully pour into freezer pop molds and freeze until solid.

YIELD: 3 cups (705 ml) mixture; number of pops will depend upon the size of your molds

Peanut Butter Cup Ice Cream

▶ **NUT**: PEANUT ▶ GLUTEN-FREE POTENTIAL ▶ SOY-FREE POTENTIAL

We're pretty sure you've heard of the craze that is aquafaba. (The liquid from a can of beans that acts similarly to egg whites when whipped.) Celine and Joni were pretty devastated when it broke the internet right AFTER *The Complete Guide to Even More Vegan Food Substitutions* went to print. So we're excited to bring a few recipes featuring the magic bean-water to you in this book!

The whipped aquafaba base makes the need for an ice-cream maker obsolete in this easy, albeit time-consuming recipe. The first part of the recipe makes a wonderful marshmallow-like fluff that is perfect as a topping for berries, and a crucial part of the Rocky Road Pie (page 170).

The resulting ice cream is soft and easy to scoop, , even after a week in the freezer. It has an almost custard-like mouthfeel . . . similar to a classic semifreddo. This recipe is peanut butter and chocolate because this is a nut book, but you can play with all sorts of flavor combos here—lemon lavender, raspberry lime, cookies and cream . . . all sorts!

1 cup (235 ml) aquafaba

1 cup (192 g) granulated raw sugar

2 teaspoons (10 ml) pure vanilla extract

¼ to ½ teaspoon cream of tartar, fresh lemon juice, or xanthan gum, as needed

¼ cup (24 g) peanut butter powder

¼ cup (20 g) unsweetened cocoa powder

1 cup (176 g) vegan chocolate chips (mini chips work lovely here)

3 tablespoons (48 g) peanut butter

1 tablespoon (14 g) coconut oil

Add the aquafaba to the bowl of your stand mixer. Using a whisk attachment, begin whipping the liquid on high speed into stiff peaks. Depending on your machine, this can take up to 30 minutes.

With the machine still running, add the sugar 1 tablespoon (12 g) at a time, incorporating it fully until all the sugar has been added. Add the vanilla, and continue to whip until shiny and smooth stiff peaks form. Again, this can take up to 30 minutes depending on your machine. Add the cream of tartar as needed for stabilization.

Stop here and you have a delicious marshmallow-y fluff perfect as a topping for desserts, berries, and pies.

Add in the peanut butter powder and cocoa powder, and continue to whip on a lower speed until fully incorporated. Your mixture may collapse slightly, and that's okay. Fold in the chocolate chips, and place in the freezer for 1 hour.

Heat the peanut butter and coconut oil in the microwave or in a small sauce pot, just until liquid so it can be poured. Remove the mixture from the freezer. Swirl in the melted peanut butter. Transfer to a freezer-safe container and freeze for several hours, or overnight.

YIELD: 32 ounces

Recipe Note

A couple of notes about working with aquafaba: Every brand and type of bean is different, and even the same brand and type may vary from can to can. It is difficult to give EXACT instruction. This recipe is pretty forgiving so you should be okay, even if this is your first foray into the magical world of bean water! Sometimes, you get a bum batch. It happens. You will know about 3 or 4 minutes into whipping that it's just not gonna fluff up. If you do not have a high-quality stand mixer, you can give your aquafaba a head start in a high-speed blender. The blender will get you about halfway there. Transfer it to the bowl of your mixer before you add any of the other ingredients and let the mixer do the rest. If you are still not getting the desired stability, even after the sugar has been added in, you may need to add in a stabilizer. Many seem to work: cream of tartar, lemon juice, vinegar, or xanthan gum. But you only need a small amount.

Nut Butter Magic Candy Ice Cream Topping

▶ **NUT**: DEPENDS UPON WHICH NUT BUTTER YOU CHOOSE ▶ QUICK AND EASY
▶ SOY-FREE POTENTIAL ▶ GLUTEN-FREE POTENTIAL

Magic Shell. We're sure you've had it at some point in your life. That magic sauce you pour over ice cream that gets hard and crunchy as soon as it hits the ice cream? Well, if you have a look at the crazy list of ingredients on that bottle, the real magic is how any of us survived eating it!

Luckily for us, there is a better way. Now we didn't come up with this idea. In fact, there are hundreds of versions of DIY Magic Shell all over the interwebs. When Joni was in Austin, she had a peanut butter version that blew her away. She asked what was in it, and was surprised to hear it had only three ingredients! Nut butter, sweetener, and coconut oil! So, if you've seen it before, we apologize, but if you are making your own homemade ice cream, why not go next level and make your own magic candy coating to top it?

½ cup (128 g) creamy nut butter

¼ cup (60 ml) coconut oil

2 tablespoons (30 ml) liquid sweetener (agave, coconut nectar, brown rice syrup, corn syrup . . .)

Add all the ingredients to a small bowl and heat just enough to easily combine. Once heated, we like to place it in a squeeze bottle, then put a finger over the hole and give it a good shake. Spoon or pour over ice cream. The liquid will harden in 30 seconds or less. It will go from shiny to dull and matte. You can tap it with your spoon and it will crack.

YIELD: Just under a cup (14 tablespoons, or 210 ml)

Rocky Road Pie

▶ **NUT**: ALMOND ▶ SOY-FREE POTENTIAL ▶ GLUTEN-FREE POTENTIAL

Rocky road has a controversial past. Walnuts, pecans, cashews, or almonds? Well, we went with almonds, but you can choose whatever nut you like! You can even mix it up if you want to. There's no wrong answer!

FOR THE PIE:

1 store-bought 9-inch (23 cm) vegan chocolate cookie pie crust

Follow the recipe for the Peanut Butter Cup Ice Cream (page 166) up to the marshmallow-y fluff stage

1 ripe avocado, mashed

12 ounces (340 g) soft silken tofu, mashed

½ cup (40 g) unsweetened cocoa powder

½ teaspoon chocolate or pure vanilla extract

2 tablespoons (16 g) cornstarch

½ cup (45 g) sliced almonds, lightly toasted

FOR THE ALMOND COCOA DRIZZLE:

½ cup (96 g) granulated raw sugar

3 tablespoons (48 g) almond butter

2 tablespoons (30 ml) almond milk

2 tablespoons (10 g) unsweetened cocoa powder

To make the pie: Remove half of the marshmallow-y fluff from your mixer bowl and place in the refrigerator. This will be your topping.

Preheat the oven to 350°F (180°C, or gas mark 4).

To the remaining marshmallow-y fluff, add in the remaining pie ingredients, except the sliced almonds, and continue to whip until it is silky smooth and resembles pudding. (I enlisted the help of my immersion blender for this.)

Pour the chocolate mixture into the pie crust. It should fill the pie crust about three-quarters full. Place on the center rack in the oven and bake for 45 minutes. Remove from the oven, and cool completely in the refrigerator for several hours to set. While cooling, make the drizzle.

To make the drizzle: Add all the ingredients to a small sauce pot. Heat over medium heat until the sugar has completely melted and a smooth sauce is formed. If, after the sugar has completely melted, you find your sauce too thick, you can add in more milk 1 tablespoon (15 ml) at a time. Remove from the heat and allow to cool.

Wait until just before serving to top off the pie. Once the pie has completely cooled and set, spread the remaining marshmallow-y fluff all over the top. If you leave your pie to cool overnight before topping, you might need to refresh your marshmallow-y fluff if it has deflated. Simply whip it for a few more minutes in your mixer until it springs back to life. Sprinkle with the toasted almonds and drizzle liberally with the Almond Cocoa Drizzle.

YIELD: One 9-inch (23 cm) pie, 8 servings

ACKNOWLEDGMENTS

At the risk of sounding like broken records after having worked with them on so many books, we want to extend our heartfelt gratitude to Fair Winds Press for putting their trust in us and lending their expertise throughout the years. With a very special mention to: Amanda Waddell, Heather Godin, Renae Haines, and Katie Fawkes. We would also like to acknowledge the hard work, talent, and dedication of Betsy Gammons, who will always remain in our hearts.

High-fives to the ever-awesome Jenna Patton for making the copy-editing process entirely pain-free!

Last but most definitely not least, thank you to our hardworking team of testers for helping us in so many ways. We couldn't do it without you, and you are the wind beneath our vegan buffalo wings: Courtney Blair, Kelly Cavalier, Shannon Davis, Monique and Michel Narbel-Gimzia, Jenna Patton (www.tastefulediting.com), Constanze Reichardt (www.seitanismymotor.com), Jody Weiner, Rochelle Krogar-West, and Liz Wyman.

ABOUT THE AUTHORS

Celine Steen is the coauthor of *Vegan Sandwiches Save the Day!*, *The Complete Guide to Even More Vegan Food Substitutions*, *The Great Vegan Grains Book*, and more. She lives in California with her husband and two demanding cats. She occasionally updates her blog, HaveCakeWillTravel.com. You can always get in touch with her at hello@celinesteen.com.

Joni Marie Newman is the author of *Fusion Food in the Vegan Kitchen*, *Vegan Food Gifts*, the co-author of *Going Vegan*, *The Complete Guide to Vegan Food Substitutions*, and more. She lives in Long Beach, California, with her husband and their furry four-legged children. She runs the blog JustTheFood.com and can be found on Twitter, Facebook, and Instagram as @JoniMarieNewman. You can e-mail her at joni@justthefood.com.

INDEX